CAST OUT

CAST OUT

A Call for a Forgiving Society in an Age of Incarceration

JOSEPH MARGULIES

BEACON PRESS, BOSTON

Beacon Press
24 Farnsworth Street
Boston, Massachusetts
www.beacon.org

Beacon Press books
are published under the auspices of
the Unitarian Universalist Association of Congregations.

Printed in the United States of America

29 28 27 26 8 7 6 5 4 3 2 1

This book is printed on acid-free paper that meets the uncoated paper ANSI/
NISO specifications for permanence as revised in 1992.

Text design by BookMatters

Library of Congress Cataloguing-in-Publication
Data is available for this title.
Hardcover ISBN: 978-0-8070-2170-5
E-book ISBN: 978-0-8070-2174-3
Audiobook: 978-0-8070-2547-5

The authorized representative in the EU for product safety and compliance is
Easy Access System Europe 16879218, Mustamäe tee 50, 10621 Tallinn, Estonia:
https://beacon.org/eu-contact.

For Sandra, who understands

If you feel pain, you are alive.
If you feel other people's pain, you are a human being.
—LEO TOLSTOY

CONTENTS

	Introduction	xi
ONE	Dispatch from a Forgiving Society	1
TWO	"This Is Eric"	11
THREE	"What the Fuck Is Wrong with This Kid?"	33
FOUR	"The Disquieting Complexity of Ourselves"	61
FIVE	"What If It's Just Human Beings?"	78
SIX	"He's Not Ready"	103
SEVEN	"He Is Not That Person Today"	125
EIGHT	The Whatabouts	144
	The Way Forward	149
	Acknowledgments	151
	Notes	155

INTRODUCTION

For many years, I have felt like a stranger in the United States. I was born here, and I've lived here all my life, but I no longer recognize this place. Much about it is still familiar. The official language is the same, the map and the calendar haven't changed, and we still celebrate the same holidays. But gradually, the United States has become unrecognizable to me.

I've tried for a very long time to put my finger on this feeling, and to put into words what began as a vague unease but is now an overwhelming sense of estrangement, and this is my conclusion: In the United States today, we celebrate cruelty and revel in the pain of others. Yes, as a country we have been cruel many times before, and yes, not everyone behaves this way. But I can't think of a time when so many people were so *enthusiastically* cruel, and when this enthusiasm for viciousness had achieved such cultural dominance.

And we are cruel in a very particular way. We live in a time when imminent and irreversible change looms over us. Climate change. Demographic change. Technological change. Not just in the United

States but around the world. From all directions, it seems as though tsunamis of indescribable power are poised to crash into us, and that the old way of navigating the world will soon be washed away. This feeling that we are balanced on the brink of something new and unrecognizable—a feeling that many people, regardless of political affiliation, find terrifying—has produced a sense of tribal desperation.

And in our desperation, in our fear of a chaotic and untamable future, many among us resort to what humans do best when they are frightened, which is to imagine monsters, erect walls, and police the boundaries of belonging. We have imprisoned ourselves in the mental cages of *us* and *them*.

Increasingly, the cultural norm in this country is spectacularly intolerant. To live in the United States today is to be immersed in a culture that is uncurious, ungenerous, and unyielding. In a word, American society is *unforgiving*, and in these pages, I ask what it will take for us to become the opposite. How can we imagine and then build a forgiving society?

I imagine a society that has neither the right nor the inclination to treat any human being as a monster, alien to the rest of us, and where no transgression, no matter how severe, permits society to dissolve the bonds that all humans share, simply because they are human. A world where public safety matters, but where punishment proceeds from the premise that wrongdoers were, are, and will always remain one of us, and where the goal of accountability is not to cast out but to bring back.

This is the world I want to live in. I come to it after (and because of) a long career defending the so-called monsters. In addition to my life as a professor, I am a criminal defense and civil rights lawyer, and for nearly four decades, I have represented people charged with or convicted of the most vicious crimes. All were poor and many were on death row. I have also been at the forefront of challenges to the government's post-9/11 detention regime and have represented people imprisoned and tortured by the United States in Guantánamo, Iraq, and secret CIA black sites all over the world.

My work has led me to a deeply personal moral philosophy, which I long ago distilled to eight words: There is no them; there is only us. If history and psychology teach us anything, it is that any of us can do monstrous things, and if all of us can be monstrous, then none of us are monsters, which is why I do not believe in the "other," the mythical creature that so many people are so quick to find and eager to expel. This philosophy links me, at a level of shared humanity, to people who have caused unimaginable pain, but also to those who have endured it. It connects me to people whose beliefs and behavior I admire a great deal, but also to those whose words and deeds I abhor. In every way that matters, I know that I am no different from them and they are no different from me.

My philosophy also supplies me with a particular view of human nature. I believe in the boundless capacity of the human spirit and am constantly in awe at the ability of people to transform themselves. Again and again, I have seen people overcome heartbreaking loss and unimaginable adversity. Likewise, I do not believe anyone is incorrigible. How could I? I have known far too many people whose present looks nothing like their past. Yet, I know this belief puts me at odds with a great many people, some of whom wield considerable power.

Stephen Miller, for instance, is President Donald Trump's deputy chief of staff. He is of the view that some people "will do nothing with their lives but rape, maim, and murder. They cannot be rehabilitated, they cannot be saved, they cannot be coached into some better way of living." And because they are irredeemable, Miller believes they must be cast out, forever. He says, "We need a place in this country where we can send people to visually demonstrate the total separation from society—the fact that they are not going to live among us and will never live among us."[1] Miller not only believes in monsters, he thinks they can be spotted, even from a safe distance of space and time. All I can say is that Stephen Miller and I see the world with very different eyes.

My focus in these pages is on people literally cast out, which is what it means to be sent to prison in this country. I draw my lessons from people in prison because it is in the treatment of prisoners that an unforgiving society reveals itself most clearly. Still, when I describe society as unforgiving, I mean much more than the workings of the criminal legal system. A bloated carceral state is a symptom of an unforgiving society, but it is not the sickness. When I decry the determination to cast people out and imprison them in their past, I do not mean simply the two million people behind bars or the five million under carceral supervision, or even the tens of millions who have a criminal record. Imprisonment takes many forms, and no one needs to spend a night in jail to feel the sting of an unforgiving society; degradation, humiliation, and ostracism have more in common with incarceration than many people care to acknowledge.

If you are content with life in our unforgiving land, then you will not like this book, since we aspire to live in very different places. But if you are attracted to the idea of a forgiving society, a society that sees us in them and them in us, then I think my book will speak to you. It is built around six people who did terrible things, and whose stories I tell in chapters 2–7. They all took different paths to the worst day of their life, but in all the ways that matter, their stories are also all the same, for they reveal the many ways an unforgiving society contrives to cast people out, all of which are equally wrong. I do not minimize or shrink from the pain they caused, and when you first learn what they did, I suspect you will feel the pull of the unforgiving society. You may believe that these six people are not one of us. My goal is to trouble that impulse, to complicate it, and to suggest another way to see the world.

But though my book is a collection of stories that show us a different way to think (and feel) about people who have committed horrific crimes, I do not view it as merely another book that rails against mass incarceration. You can read it that way, and if you did, I would not view the book as a failure. But that is not my goal. My goal is much larger. To me, the way we treat people in prison, especially those who have caused the greatest harm, is not only the clearest example of our unforgiving society but also the greatest challenge to those who would undo it. If society cannot cast out those who terrorize a neighborhood, who can it cast out? If those who take an innocent life are not "them," who is? My answer is no one, and my goal is to prove it.

But first, we glimpse what a forgiving society might look like.

CHAPTER 1

DISPATCH FROM A FORGIVING SOCIETY

Shortly after the January 6, 2021, riot at the US Capitol, the press began to run articles with the ostensible goal of painting a more complete picture of the insurrectionists. On January 18, the *New York Times* profiled Klete Keller, the former Olympic swimmer who participated in the riot and was later charged with various offenses.[1]

The article paints the 6'6" Keller as a gentle giant. Former coaches and teammates recalled him as a "champion prankster" with "a foghorn laugh" who "lived to be liked." But those who knew him best described "a melancholy side" that overtook him once his athletic career ended. "Great person, great soul, great teammate," said one of his fellow Olympic swimmers. "But he just had a hard time finding his place in society outside the pool." Attempts to build a new career "didn't pan out." His marriage collapsed, and an ugly divorce kept him from his three children "for long periods." Without work and with no place to go, he spent months living out of his car, maintaining a membership at a local gym so he could have a place to shower.

Yet the core of the article was not the difficulty Keller has had since he retired from competitive swimming. It was the deep, searing regret he felt over his involvement in the riot. The profile opens with a dramatic scene. One of Keller's former coaches called him after learning he had been part of the mob and was surprised when Keller, "the decorated swimmer he had known as a merry prankster," dissolved into tears. "He apologized to me," the former coach said. "He kept repeating, 'You've done so much for me, and I let you down.' He kept saying over and over, 'I didn't mean for any of this to happen.'" The article closes on the same apologetic note. Another former coach, who spoke with Keller the day he appeared in court, recalled that he "cried throughout their 15-minute conversation." He said Keller "never thought about what could happen. He was at the wrong place, at the wrong time, with the wrong people." In the article's nearly 1,600 words, the first and last image for the reader is a sobbing, remorseful Keller, whose role in this riot is shriveled almost to nothing, more accidental than intentional.

And while the article is long on apologies and personal history, it makes no mention of the nearly 140 officers injured in the riot, including one who, according to the chairman of the Capitol Police officers union, suffered two cracked ribs and two crushed discs and another who was stabbed "with a metal fence stake."[2] Nor does the profile remind the reader of the police officer who suffered two strokes and died within twenty-four hours of being attacked at the Capitol, the two officers who responded to the riot and later took their own lives, the woman who was shot and killed inside the Capitol, the woman who was trampled to death on the steps outside, or the members of Congress who barely escaped the melee.[3] In fact, the *only* mention of the riot treats the victims as abstractions: "crowds ... assaulted the Capitol," and a "mob [was] bent on disrupting ... democracy."

Thus, on the front page of the paper of record, we are treated to a lengthy profile of a criminal defendant that trains the reader's sole attention on a wholly sympathetic portrayal of the accused, minimizes his legal and moral culpability in the crime, downplays the seriousness of the offense, and ignores the injuries suffered by the victims. To put it gently, this is not the norm for crime reporting, most of which simply repeats information supplied by the police. One person stabbed another in a restaurant after an argument over $10. Somebody shot someone else after an argument in a hotel. Offenders are stick figures. Trying to understand the people described in these snippets is like trying to describe the taste of sand.

But if the profile of Keller is not crime reporting, what is it? The Capitol riot was widely described as an attack on "the people's house." In a very real sense, Keller committed a wrong against all of us, and his profile in the *Times* invites all of us to join in reclaiming his good name and his place in society. The profile of Klete Keller is a public plea that society judge him and his behavior in a spirit of forgiveness.

We tend to think of forgiveness as a purely private affair, but the *Times* profile shows that it can also be a social act. Personal and social forgiveness have much in common, but they are not the same thing. Both begin with a wrong. Some wrongs are primarily personal (I cheat on my wife) and some are primarily public (I cheat on my taxes), but most are both. The mob at the Capitol, for instance, injured specific people (a personal wrong), but it also attacked the integrity of the democratic process (a public wrong).

Just as society can be wronged, it can be forgiving. We all know people we would describe as unforgiving. They detect slights where none were intended; they can't let go of a grievance, no matter how minor; they tend to dismiss or discount explanations, no matter how compelling; and they set conditions on forgiveness that are out of proportion to the harm they suffered. Likewise, we all know people we would say are forgiving, which generally implies just the opposite. And though we are not accustomed to thinking in these terms, a group—no less than an individual—can be unforgiving in much the same way. It can dwell obsessively on objectively minor infractions, cast out wrongdoers despite compelling explanations, hold onto grievances long beyond any morally defensible justification, and make a wrongdoer jump through endless, unreasonable hoops as a condition to reclaiming their place in the group. A forgiving society, by contrast, adopts the attitude displayed in the *Times* profile of Klete Keller—an attitude of benevolent, empathetic compassion undergirded by the foundational belief that the person is not an alien or a monster, but one of us, a flawed soul who strayed, as all of us might stray.

Some people balk at the idea of a forgiving society because they think it will bring well-deserved punishment to a premature end—or worse, that it will preclude punishment altogether. But a forgiving society may still insist on accountability. If I injure someone, she might forgive me unconditionally, but she also might insist that I first make things right. She might demand an apology, for instance, or that I otherwise make amends. In the same way, society might forgive a wrongdoer unconditionally, but more likely, it will insist that they first make things right. It might insist, in other words, on accountability.

In an unforgiving society—that is, in our society—this accountability is often vindictive and vengeful. It seems designed to mark the wrongdoer as unworthy and to permanently cast them out. In a forgiving society, accountability aims for something very different. A forgiving society will not judge someone until it struggles to understand both the act and the actor in all their complexity. To judge in a forgiving spirit does not mean closing our eyes to the pain that a person caused or the harm they have done. It demands that the wrong be neither minimized nor exaggerated, neither sensationalized nor diminished. When reflecting on the crime that landed them in prison, people behind bars have often said to me, "What happened, happened." The crime exists as a brute, unalterable fact that they cannot undo and will never forget. But they, and all of us, can endeavor to understand it, which means struggling to make sense not simply of what they did but why they did it. The effort to understand why one of us has done something horribly wrong, and to accept that while the wrong may cost them their liberty, it will never sever the bonds that all humans share and will not deprive them of their membership in society, is the hallmark of a forgiving society.

Frankly, judgment in a forgiving spirit is not as strange as it sounds; we do it automatically for the people we know and love. When someone close to us blunders, no matter how badly, we mentally supply an explanation based on what we know of their past and their struggles. This explanation helps us make sense of behavior that might otherwise be incomprehensible, or wholly at odds with the person we know. Perhaps our explanation is correct, perhaps it is not, but as a rule, we do not suppose that those close to us act for no reason at all. We take it as a given that there is *some* explanation. And we supply this explanation because we believe that those close to us are one of us. They are not monsters who do horrible things for no reason. This is what Keller's friends and coaches were trying to say, probably without conscious thought. They were saying, in so many words, "You have to understand. He's not who you think he is. He just got caught up in something that he never intended." This is the language of a forgiving society. They are *not* saying Keller should escape responsibility for what he did; nothing in the profile suggests that any of them believe that. It's just that he should be judged as one of us and not part of a mythical "them."

Social forgiveness acts as an orientation or an attitude. It is not a set of rules. Instead, it is the state of mind that a group brings to those who have committed a wrong, providing a background sense for the moral worth of the person who strayed and exerting a powerful influence on everything that society does. It affects the language used to describe them and the process employed to hold them accountable. If they are brought into the criminal legal system, it will affect the charges they might face, the procedures used to adjudicate their guilt, and the kind and quality of punishment they receive. But most of all, to approach a wrongdoer in a spirit of forgiveness means that accountability will always be leavened by the certainty that they were and will always remain part of the group. More than that, it means the purpose of accountability is not to cast them out forever but to create a society where victims or survivors are made whole and wrongs like this never happen again.

Social forgiveness differs from personal forgiveness in one critical respect. Personal forgiveness is a private gift that a victim may grant or withhold as she sees fit. But social forgiveness is a public good that determines how a transgressor will be treated by society. And like any public good, it is doled out unevenly. Researchers have identified three behaviors that most reliably activate what the social psychologist Michael McCullough calls "the forgiveness instinct": apology, self-abasement, and compensation. Presented with these behaviors, our attitude toward a transgressor softens noticeably. We become less vengeful, less apt to view them as outsiders, and less eager to see them punished.[4]

Consider how these features play out in the profile of Klete Keller. While the article makes no mention of compensation—I haven't seen anything to suggest that Keller, or any rioter, has offered to pay for the damage and the pain they caused, though everyone convicted in the riot is fined $2,000 for damage to the Capitol—the *Times* article supplies a textbook example of apology and self-abasement. At least according to his coaches, Keller apologized unequivocally, with no attempt to deflect responsibility or place blame onto others. And his is not the reluctant apology of the unrepentant ("I'm sorry if my actions upset you"). At the same time, the image of his uncontrollable sobbing in two separate conversations functions as a display of self-abasing behavior.

All of this sends powerful signals to the rest of society. To begin with, Keller's behavior reaffirms his attachment to the values and norms of the group. By acknowledging that he has done wrong, he declares his commitment to play by the rules in the future. This serves as both a plea that he not be cast out as a pariah and a reassurance that he poses no threat. By his actions, in other words, he says, "I am one of you, I can be trusted despite this lapse, I am not dangerous." This portrait is then reinforced by the editorializing of his friends and coaches. The people "who know [him] best" found it "nothing less than bizarre" to see him at the Capitol and made a determined effort to diminish his culpability. Keller, they said, "didn't mean for any of this to happen," "never thought about what could happen," and was simply "at the wrong place, at the wrong time, with the wrong people." These statements defang Keller's behavior by draining it of its purposefulness. And his wracking torment—the picture of him sobbing—activates the sense of empathy that many people feel when faced with the suffering of others. Empathy is a primary pathway to forgiveness.[5]

As much as his apology and abasement help Keller in his quest to be forgiven, they are not the only things that work in his favor. There is, perhaps above all, the matter of his race. Keller is white, and a picture of him appeared in the article. His whiteness likely lends his plea at least an implicit boost. Researchers have long found that white people tend to associate blackness (but not whiteness) with criminality and to believe that Black people are more prone to violence than white people. As the psychologist Jennifer Eberhardt and her colleagues have observed, the "mere presence of a Black man...can trigger thoughts that he is violent and criminal."[6] In short, some people are apt to view Keller empathetically simply by virtue of his race.

Keller also benefited from his social status. He is not simply an average Joe, an arbitrary middle-aged white man. He swam in three Olympic games and won two gold medals alongside the storied Michael Phelps. In the United States, there are few titles that are more universally honored than "Olympian." Even the titles that often confer the most status and respect in today's society—physician, first responder—do not conjure the same image of talent, dedication, sacrifice, and patriotism. In these fractious times, even soldiers may not stir the same feelings, particularly as news came out of the many veterans who participated in the riot at the Capitol.[7] Perhaps more than anyone else, Olympians are revered as American heroes—or as the *Times* put it, "the personification...of American greatness and success."

Keller's rarefied perch makes his story irresistible. The media always loves an Icarus tale: How could someone who flew so high fall so low? But more than that, Keller's status magnifies the impact of his tearful, heartfelt apology. Psychologists have found that people tend to be particularly impressed with apologies by high-status offenders and are more apt to forgive their transgressions than those of people who do not enjoy the same social status. Though Keller no doubt behaved the same as many other rioters, his apology touches many people more deeply precisely because it comes from a place of privilege.[8]

Then there is the benefit that Keller enjoys from the people who vouch for him. As a former elite swimmer, Keller had an entire retinue of well-educated, well-spoken ex-teammates and ex-coaches who could be reached in fairly short order. They could be counted on to flesh out Keller's profile, disclose his backstory, and give voice to his great regret. Through their recollections, Keller becomes more than a caricature. He becomes a complex human being, as flawed, frail, and damaged as the rest of us. But it is important to recognize that their recollections are carefully curated—either by the journalist who wrote the article or her sources—to create a favorable impression. The journalist either did not speak to Keller's ex-wife (she of the contentious divorce) or elected not to quote what she said, and seems to have made no effort to figure out why he was denied contact with his children for so long. For his part, Keller declined to speak with the journalist.

In recounting all this, I do not wish Keller ill. I hope he receives a nuanced, compassionate assessment of his moral culpability, informed by the fact that his actions on that single, fateful day are not the whole of his existence. I hope that assessment considers the regret he feels and the pain he endures. In short, I hope he is judged in a spirit of forgiveness. But my ambition for a forgiving society means I have the exact same hope for everyone who has committed a great wrong and been cast out for what they cannot change, regardless of whether it was a crime. Everyone whose inexcusable behavior led bewildered friends and grief-stricken family to mutter that same tired trilogy—wrong place, wrong time, wrong people. They too are one of us, and they should all be judged in the same spirit of compassionate forgiveness as Klete Keller.

But they won't. Researchers have consistently found that many people who've been dragged into the criminal legal system regret what they have done and, like Keller, want to apologize to their victims and be forgiven. As the journalist Elizabeth Bruenig put it, they seek a world where they are not compelled to "permanently inhabit [their] failure."[9] Yet few indeed can ever hope to see their regret empathetically displayed to an audience in the tens of millions. Fewer still can hope that it be communicated by such well-respected spokesmen. Perhaps none at all can hope, in their wildest dreams, that their regret will be unsullied by ugly reminders of the pain they helped inflict. And literally none start with the built-in advantage that comes from being a white Olympic champion. The pedestal on which Keller stands is a monument to the grossly unjust politics of social forgiveness.

And this injustice will endure until we change our approach. It will endure until we accept that those who commit grave wrongs are not the demons we imagine them to be. Until we acknowledge that they too are one of us. Once we embrace this difficult and painful truth, we will have taken the first and most important step toward the creation of a forgiving society. To approach each person in a spirit of forgiveness rather than vengeance—regardless of what they have done—and to treat them as a member of society rather than an outcast will slowly unwind the punitive turn of the past sixty years.

Because the privileges of race and class are so deeply embedded in American life, I recognize that someone like Keller will receive what is stubbornly withheld from so many. But that is not his fault, and society should not cast him out simply because it wrongly casts out others. Justice is never served by being unjust, and cruelty is not made less cruel simply because it balances out cruelty inflicted elsewhere. The road to a forgiving society demands that we widen the reach of compassion, not ration it.

Keller pleaded guilty in September 2021 to a single count of obstruction of Congress. In exchange for his guilty plea, six other counts against him were dismissed. After he was arrested and charged, Keller cooperated with the government's investigation. At his sentencing in December 2023, prosecutors asked the judge to sentence him to ten months in prison, less than the fifteen to twenty-one months called for by the federal sentencing guidelines. The judge declined and sentenced him to three years of probation, which included six months of home detention and 360 hours of community service. "If ever there was a case that screamed out for probation, this is it," the judge said.[10]

CHAPTER 2

"THIS IS ERIC"

> The Grand Jurors of the State of Louisiana, duly impaneled and sworn in and for the body of the Parish of Orleans . . . present that Eric Matthews, late of the Parish of Orleans, on the 12th day of May in the year of our Lord, one thousand, nine hundred ninety-four in the Parish of Orleans . . . committed First Degree Murder of GLENIECE EVERETTE, age TWO (2) years old.
>
> —INDICTMENT, *State of Louisiana v. Eric Matthews* (1994)

If your mental vision of a prison is a windowless fortress with high walls ringed by razor wire, get that out of your head. The Louisiana State Penitentiary is not a building. It's not even a cluster of buildings. It's an enormous, sprawling prison farm that sits in a bend of the Mississippi River and stretches for miles across the steaming fields of Tunica, Louisiana, an hour north of Baton Rouge. It's the largest maximum-security prison in the country. The idea of eighteen thousand acres doesn't mean a lot to me, but you get some sense for its size when you consider that you could put the entire island of

Manhattan inside the prison and still have more than a square mile of unused space. Officially, it's the Louisiana State Penitentiary, but everyone calls it Angola.

Before it was a prison, Angola was a slave plantation—or rather, seven contiguous plantations, one of which was named Angola because that's the kingdom where the majority of the slaves came from. Over time, the whole property came to be known as the Angola Plantation, probably because that's where the slave owners built their mansion. The State of Louisiana bought the site in 1901, and it's been the home of the Louisiana State Penitentiary ever since.[1] So far as I can tell, there is no clamor to rename the prison, where three in four prisoners are Black, nearly all of whom will die behind bars.

When Eric Matthews arrived at Angola in December 1994, the prison bus rolled to a stop and a correctional officer (CO) shuffled him off the bus and onto the prison grounds for the first time, shackled at his hands and feet. He looked around at the boundless expanse and in a daze asked himself, "How on earth did I get here?" If he had asked that question out loud, anyone at the prison would've been happy to repeat what the trial court pronounced after the jury found him guilty of murdering two-year-old Gleniece "Christina" Everette: "The Defendant is to spend the rest of his natural life in the Department of Corrections without the benefit of probation, parole, or suspension of sentence."

But the answer to Eric's question began long before a judge sentenced him to life imprisonment.

1.

Great cities do not collapse all at once. It is not for nothing that writers describe cities as they would a living thing, with a heart and soul powerful enough to sustain all that a healthy city does—thousands of businesses; hundreds of schools and places of worship; countless restaurants and taverns; scores of theaters, concert halls, and stadiums; newspapers, and radio and television stations; hospitals and clinics; an airport, a train station, a bus depot; and all supported by a government that collects the trash, cleans the streets, maintains the parks, delivers the mail, purifies the water, supplies the electricity, patrols the neighborhoods, and settles the disputes. A great city cannot be felled by a single blow. New York City recovered quickly from the attacks of September 11, 2001, just as Los Angeles will quickly recover from the wildfires of 2025. A great city is *resilient*.

But even a great city is not indestructible. When businesses leave by the score; when thousands of people move away and those who stay can't find good work and can't pay their bills; when houses empty and lots are weed-choked; when children with nothing to do start breaking windows and vandalizing buildings; when no one is paying taxes and the government runs out of money and can't replace the streetlights or fix the potholes or collect the trash or pay its teachers or protect its residents; when people live from one relief check to the next and addiction starts to make sense; when dealing drugs and selling your body seem like the surest ways to make a living—when it all goes to hell, even a great city falls apart.

Cities do not collapse by accident. Jobs do not simply appear or disappear, as if by magic. There are reasons why cities thrive and decline, and behind these reasons, there are winners and losers. Like other major cities in the United States, New Orleans thrived during the Second World War because jobs were plentiful and comparatively well-paid. Whites and Blacks alike thronged to the city from the surrounding countryside to work in the factories and the port. Though whites in the Jim Crow South always had access to the best public and private jobs, and though many employers simply refused to hire Blacks, the rising tide of wartime production lifted all boats. It just lifted white boats a lot higher.[2]

But all that began to change in the decades after the war. Postwar suburbanization transformed New Orleans, just as it did other major cities, beginning a process that ended in the city's long decline. Nearly everything about suburbanization favored whites over Blacks. Thousands of high-paying industrial jobs in the suburbs were opened to whites but not Blacks. As one legal scholar would later write, "Up and down the Mississippi River outside the city lay oil refineries and chemical factories with largely white work forces."[3] Whites in the city could also access low-interest mortgages that were denied to Blacks, and that in many cases made it cheaper to buy a home in the suburbs than rent an apartment in the city. This allowed an entire generation of whites, but not Blacks, to tap into the wealth-creating engine of home ownership. And even if Black professionals had the money to buy a suburban home, for many years the suburbs themselves were closed to them.[4]

Economically, the suburbs' gain was the city's loss. The deindustrialization of New Orleans began in the early 1950s and continued throughout most of the second half of the twentieth century. Blacks in the city were hit particularly hard. Shut out of work in the expanding suburbs and excluded from the best municipal jobs, Black unemployment and underemployment in New Orleans began to rise in the '50s and continued to climb for the remainder of the century. The deepest cut may have been the mechanization of the port. Longshoreman was one of the few stable and well-paid jobs open to Blacks in New Orleans, but beginning in 1956, containerization transformed the industry by sharply reducing the need for labor. Between the 1960s and 1980s, the number of longshoremen fell by 75 percent nationwide, and hundreds of Black longshoremen in New Orleans were thrown out of work.[5] By 1970, while the great majority of Black men in the city were employed, their average annual wage was barely more than half the average annual wage of a white man.[6] Though this wage disparity improved slightly over the next three decades, those improvements were swamped by the number of Black men who left the labor force entirely. By 2000, nearly 30 percent of the Black men in New Orleans were either unemployed or out of the work force.[7]

As jobs disappeared, crime rose. Beginning in the 1950s and continuing through the '70s, heroin played a major part in this increase, as Black dealers took over the market from the Italian Mafia and plied their trade in and around the segregated public housing projects. As early as the mid-1950s, heroin addiction was concentrated almost entirely in the increasingly impoverished Black neighborhoods. In the 1960s, violent crime began to increase dramatically, as addiction combined with poverty to produce desperation. By 1966, New Orleans had the highest per capita murder rate in the nation.[8]

And it kept getting worse. In 1968, the Fair Housing Act opened the suburbs to Blacks who could afford to rent or buy outside the city, which meant that many New Orleans neighborhoods, including the public housing projects, became the site of concentrated and deeply entrenched poverty. Using data from the 1970 census, researchers calculated that New Orleans was the poorest of America's fifty largest cities.[9] As poverty got worse, so did crime. Throughout the 1970s and mid-1980s, the murder rate in New Orleans was twice as high as in US cities of comparable size. In the five years after 1988, the murder rate in New Orleans soared to triple that of comparable US cities.[10] In 1994, New Orleans suffered through 424 murders, including high-profile killings by two different New Orleans police officers as the city once again became the murder capital of the country. On the day Eric killed Christina, there were six other homicides in New Orleans, making it the bloodiest day in the bloodiest year in the city's history.[11]

The final nail in the city's coffin was the political decimation of its tax base. As jobs and people fled to the suburbs, the city's tax base shriveled. Yet, when Louisiana rewrote its constitution in 1974 to remove the legal vestiges of Jim Crow, property owners paid no taxes on the first $50,000 of property value, which meant that nearly 80 percent of New Orleans homeowners paid no property tax and another 10 percent paid less than $100 a year.[12] As a result, New Orleans had to lean ever more heavily on state and federal funding. In 1971, the state and federal governments supplied just over 20 percent of the city's budget. A decade later, the year Ronald Reagan took office, that percentage had more than doubled.[13] But the Reagan administration cut direct and indirect federal aid to cities by 60 percent.[14] For New Orleans, these cuts could not have come at a worse time, as the oil bust of the 1980s devastated the broader Louisiana economy just as cities across the country, including New Orleans, were hit by the AIDS epidemic, the crack epidemic, and the homelessness crisis.[15]

Suburbanization and ghettoization in New Orleans thus took place in parallel, as whites and the Black middle class gradually left the city, leaving behind a Black community that was increasingly impoverished and segregated into neighborhoods that were among the most violent in the country, in a city that was systematically starved of the resources it needed to serve its residents.[16] By the time Eric Matthews was born in 1973, New Orleans was well on its way to becoming one of the most distressed cities in the country.

2.

Eric grew up near the St. Thomas Housing Projects, a cluster of low-rise apartments and townhomes that covered about twenty square blocks of the Irish Channel neighborhood in the Lower Garden District. Opened in 1941 and expanded in 1952, St. Thomas was among the first public housing projects in New Orleans. In the Jim Crow South, St. Thomas was built for low-income whites but was gradually opened to Blacks as whites left the city.[17] By the time Eric was born, St. Thomas was one of the most segregated and impoverished neighborhoods in New Orleans. In 1970, nearly three in four St. Thomas residents were Black, and nearly seven in ten lived below the federal poverty line.[18]

When legitimate work disappears, illicit work takes its place. The heroin epidemic had ebbed by 1980 but was soon replaced by crack, which ravaged New Orleans from the mid-1980s into the first decade of the new century, bringing with it unprecedented levels of addiction and violence.[19] In the 1980s, Sister Helen Prejean lived just outside the St. Thomas projects at Hope House and described what she saw in her book, *Dead Man Walking*: "Not death row, exactly, but close. Death is rampant here—from guns, disease, addiction." Between 1987 and 1991, the tenants at St. Thomas reported 48 murders, 27 rapes, 370 robberies, and 638 assaults—and violent crime is notoriously underreported. Residents boarded their windows to protect themselves from stray bullets, and parents warned their children to watch TV lying on the floor. In 1991, St. Thomas was the most violent housing project in the city.[20]

Though Eric was raised a couple of blocks from the edge of the projects, his streets still felt the effects. The sidewalk across from his doorstep was an open-air drug market, and every Friday evening, he recalled, there was "a baller's meeting," meaning a gathering of "all the guys who sold weight, wholesalers who had people working for them." Gunplay was a regular affair in his neighborhood. "We used to call them shootouts. In school you'd say, 'Oh man, there was a shootout. So and so got shot.' But you mind your business. You didn't want to seem like you knew the people." His grandmother's house, next to his own, was once shot up by mistake.

Children in violent neighborhoods often say that *their* streets are relatively safe, and that regardless of what the official statistics show, as long as they stay on this block and go in those stores and play in that park during these hours, they'll probably be okay. And much of the time, they are. But they pay a steep price for this sense of imagined safety. In violent neighborhoods, residents become attuned to the small, nearly imperceptible signs that something is about to pop off. As Eric told me in one of our visits, drifting in and out of the present tense as though part of him were still there, "Walking in the neighborhood, there's never *not* some level of tension. There was never a time that you let your guard down. I've always thought that something could go down on any day."

Without being taught, children in these neighborhoods learn that their safety depends on the ability to detect immediately and react instantly to subtle changes in the neighborhood's temperature. The knot of old men drinking wine on the street corner who suddenly fall silent, toss each other a knowing glance, then wordlessly fold up their chairs and disappear. The mothers who summon their children inside, calmly at first but with increasing urgency as the street empties. The carload of young men that inches down the street. Children are always on the alert, with at least one ear and one eye on the street, no matter what they're doing or who they're with. They know where they are at all times, how far they are from safety if they need to run, and how long it would take to get there.

And even when children develop these skills, the fact is that in places like St. Thomas, neighborhood violence is often sudden and unpredictable. In 1989, five-year-old Coco Vessel, a friend of the nuns at Hope House, was playing in a courtyard of the St. Thomas homes when one neighbor shot at another and killed Coco instead.[21] In 1992, four-year-old Eric Boyd was shot and killed in a different St. Thomas courtyard. He had just stepped outside when gunfire erupted. His family yelled for him to duck but he didn't react quickly enough.[22] In 1993, a study of young children in another New Orleans housing project found that over half the children ages nine to twelve had been victims of violence, and more than nine in ten had witnessed it.

When the researchers asked the children to draw pictures of "what happens" in their neighborhood, the children "drew in graphic detail pictures of shootings, drug deals, stabbings, fighting, and funerals, and reported being scared of the violence and of something happening to them."[23] The next year, nine-year-old James Darby, who lived in a New Orleans project, wrote a letter to President Clinton. "I want you to stop the killing in the city. I think somebody might kill me. I'm asking you nicely to stop it. I know you can do it." Nine days later, as he was walking home from a Mother's Day picnic, Darby was shot in the head and killed.[24]

This constant exposure to violence inflicts a toll that no child should endure. The stress is exhausting—the weariness in body and spirit that comes from being in a chronic state of high alert. All of us experience some level of stress in our daily lives, but this is many orders of magnitude more severe and more debilitating. Over time, the belief that the world around you is unsafe and that you are powerless to make it otherwise, the fear that any day might be the last for you or someone you love, actually changes a child's brain. The portion of their brain that alerts them to danger—warning them to fight, flee, or freeze—switches on *and stays on*.[25]

For short periods, this hypervigilance can help keep a child safe. But no one should live with the switch on all the time. Eventually, they may discover they don't know how to turn it off. They don't even know where the switch is and lack the psychological tools to find it. In this way, childhood exposure to violence reaches through time. It not only changes the way a child copes with the world but alters how they respond to stress as an adult. Conditions that a person with an undamaged brain would find merely annoying can seem life-threatening to an adult who grew up surrounded by unpredictable but potentially lethal violence. Part of their brain tells them it's *always* time to fight, flee, or freeze.[26]

To be sure, environment is not destiny, and not every child raised in a place like St. Thomas ends up in prison. The extent to which a child is damaged by this chaos depends a great deal on the cumulative impact of all the traumas they have endured. Early trauma seems to matter more than later; trauma accompanied by betrayal cuts more deeply than trauma alone; trauma to friends and family does more damage than trauma to strangers.[27] That is why it matters so much that when Eric was seven, he was molested by a family friend, a sexual assault that produced an enduring shame. Why it matters that his parents split up when he was young, that his mother drifted from one abusive boyfriend to the next, and that one of his earliest memories is of his mother being beaten by the boyfriend of the moment. Why it matters that he felt so angry and powerless when his mother woke him as a young teen and told him she had just been battered again. Why it matters that gun violence was not merely "out there" in the neighborhood. When he was fourteen, he and a boy he knew were standing outside a corner market when the child was gunned down. When he was sixteen, a neighbor shot at him after a disagreement over a bicycle. When he was twenty, a man mistook him for someone else, chased him down the street, cornered him, put a gun to his face, and pulled the trigger three times. It misfired and Eric escaped.[28]

The impact of this chaos also depends on whether a child has the opportunity to process what they endure.[29] That is why it matters so much that Eric did not tell anyone that he had been molested until many years later when he shared the story with a friend in prison. Why it matters that the person who molested him was a friend of the family, who had been invited into the home. Why it matters that he went to school the day after he was molested, the day after an acquaintance was killed at his side, and the day after a neighbor shot at him over a bicycle, as though it were just another day. Why it matters that there were no counselors or psychologists at Eric's schools, no trained professionals with whom he could share his anger and unburden his shame. These are not isolated events in a child's life. They cumulate and compound; each new trauma amplifies the last, deepening the scar and intensifying the effect.[30]

Sometimes, this cumulative trauma blocks out the person who would otherwise emerge. To appearances, Eric was the family jokester, the wonder boy who made everyone laugh as he skated above life's scarred surface, effortlessly avoiding the snares that trapped so many other young Black boys and men. He sang in the choir at the Baptist church, went to Sunday school, tutored friends at school, ran track, excelled in martial arts, and graduated fifth in his high school class. After high school, he joined the Louisiana National Guard, served as a surgical technician at Fort Polk, and was honorably discharged. He attended Bible study on Tuesdays, a youth group on Fridays, and services on Sundays. To this day, Eric has never smoked weed, never used cocaine or heroin, has only tasted alcohol occasionally, and has gotten drunk exactly once. At the time of his arrest, he was a deacon in the church, had never been arrested, and had no criminal record of any kind.[31] In a world of so much bleak despair, Eric was everyone's shining hope. To those who thought they knew him, nothing about the crime made sense.

It made no sense because friends and family saw only what Eric let them see. They didn't see his rage and didn't know his shame. Eric was a wire stretched taut. If traffic moved too slowly, his pupils dilated and he slammed the steering wheel. If a neighbor glanced at him sideways, his muscles coiled and his pulse quickened. If a stranger bumped him on the street, he clenched his fists and braced for a fight. As a teenager, Eric worked out for hours at a time, hoping that exhaustion would loosen the wire and relieve the pressure. When he was stationed at Fort Sam Houston, he joined a fight club and beat people up for money, looking for that same relief. But strategies like these worked only so well, and sometimes they didn't work at all. Inevitably, the wire would snap and his rage and shame would vent in volcanic outbursts—randomly, in response to trivial provocations or to nothing at all. Eric once beat a man senseless at a friend's wedding when he thought the man was hitting on his girlfriend. He beat up a man he saw urinating against his house. He charged after a man who cut him off in traffic. Explosive overreactions like these are all too common among adults who grew up in a world where the switch was never off. Afterward, Eric couldn't understand his reaction and was ashamed of himself. These outbursts were not all of who he was, but for brief flashes, they were all he could be.

In 1993, Eric started going out with Joanna Everette. Joanna had a two-year-old daughter, Gleniece, who everyone called Christina and who Eric loved as he would his own child. Friends and family thought Eric and Joanna were a sweet couple. They doted on each other and on Christina. In the summer of 1993, they moved in together. Though they were in their early twenties, they planned to get married. On May 12, 1994, Eric and Joanna went to the clerk's office to pick up a copy of their marriage license. They were so excited about it, they stopped off at Little St. John Missionary Baptist Church to show the pastor the license and gushed about their plans for their life together. Everything seemed perfect.

After the visit, Eric dropped Joanna off at work, and he and Christina went to Rally's to pick up a bite for lunch. They returned home, and as Eric would later recall, "by the time we arrived, I was tired. I sat on the floor dozing while Christina ate some French fries." He woke up and saw Christina smearing her fries into the carpet. The wire tightened. "I told her to stop and just eat the fries." She started to eat them again, and Eric once again dozed off. When he woke up, she was doing it again, coloring the carpet with her fries. The wire tightened and strained. "Again, I instructed her to eat them and not to waste them. I grew very impatient and irritated." And when he dozed off again and woke up a third time to see the same thing, the wire was so tight it quivered. He ordered her to get ready for a bath, and when she protested and refused, the wire snapped. "I lost it. I began to whip her with my belt. The more she cried, the more I beat her. It was as if my rage was fueled by Christina's cries."[32]

He can't explain why he reached for his belt, "except that I was whipped with a belt as a child." But he'd never whipped her before and knows he "should not have been whipping her at all, and certainly not in anger." But he couldn't stop himself. "Though I knew she was crying, at some point I could no longer hear it. And though Christina ultimately died at the hospital, I whipped the life out of this adorable little girl. It wasn't until hearing a voice in me say, 'Eric, that's enough,' that I actually stopped."[33] When Eric came to his senses and saw what he had done, he panicked, rushed Christina to the hospital, and lied. He said she had drowned in the bathtub. The hospital staff knew immediately that this was untrue. Eric was arrested that day and charged with capital murder.

3.

There's only one way to reach Angola. A two-lane country road winds twenty-two miles northwest from St. Francisville and ends at the prison's front gate. Angola is literally the end of the road. When visitors arrive, they are scanned and screened, then transported by bus to one of the many camps scattered throughout the prison. For most of the time I visited him, Eric was at the main prison. We met in a massive square room with high walls, fluorescent lights, concrete floors, and terrible acoustics. People sit at small tables in red, plastic chairs and raise their voices to be heard over the din, or lean in close, risking the ire of guards, who watch for forbidden contact.

Along three walls, prison organizations sell food and drinks, but because no prisoner can handle money, transactions require a complicated dance. You order food from a vendor, who looks to be in his mid-fifties and has probably been imprisoned in Angola for many years. He gives you a ticket, which you carry to a correctional officer in a pen enclosed in plexiglass. You pay the CO, who stamps your ticket, which you then carry back to the vendor, who makes your food. Every organization prepares something different. You get your salad over here, your burger there, your pizza at the end of the aisle. This vendor for coffee and dessert, that one for water. Within the visiting area, people can move about freely, and a visitor can stay for several hours before the COs hustle you out.

When Eric arrived in 1994, Angola richly deserved its reputation as the bloodiest prison in America. It has since lost that distinction, thanks mostly to reforms implemented by the former warden, Burl Cain, who now leads the Department of Corrections in neighboring Mississippi. But reforms or not, Angola remains a maximum-security prison, with all that implies: control, tension, risk, temptation, surveillance, boredom, and violence. Even in a well-run prison, human beings live in cages and guards reduce people to numbers. When I visited Eric, I had to memorize his prisoner ID number because there is another Black man named Eric Matthews serving a life sentence at Angola, and some of the guards couldn't keep them straight. No one thrives in prison, though some, with great effort, can carve out something like a life.

Prior to his trial, Eric met his court-appointed lawyer precisely twice. The first time was when he was charged with capital murder; the second was the first day of a trial that lasted only three. For many years, Eric thought the jury had voted 11–1 for death. Because the law in Louisiana requires that a death sentence be unanimous, the lone holdout saved his life—or so he believed. He's not sure where he got this idea but seems to remember it came from his lawyer. Wherever it came from, it's wrong. In the course of reporting this chapter, I tracked down the former lead prosecutor at Eric's trial, who told me he had saved his copy of the verdict sheets in part because, even decades later, he could not forget Eric's case. Former National Guard, church deacon, no criminal record? The case made no sense to him. He emailed the verdict sheets to me, and it turns out eight jurors had voted for life and only four voted for death. But Eric had been in prison twenty-eight years before he learned this, and the belief that he had been saved by a single juror had been a constant source of motivation. "If a single person saw me at my very worst, when all they knew about me was the absolute worst thing I had ever done and ever could do, and they still thought my life was worth saving, then it meant that one person could make a difference. One person could change somebody's life. I resolved to be that person with everyone I met in prison."

Resolutions like this are easy to make but hard to keep. Every day, Eric is tormented by the brutality of his crime. He can still recall sitting in the Orleans Parish Jail awaiting trial when an account of the murder came on the news. He sat and sobbed, horrified by what he had done. If he allowed it, the memory of his crime, and of the innocent life he took, would crush him. More than once he has thought he deserved to be crushed, and if it were only his life at stake, he told me he might have let that happen. But giving up would have dishonored the memory of the imagined juror who believed in Eric. It would prevent him from seeing the value in himself and others, as the juror saw in him.

The best prison officials understand what the outside world doesn't: When it comes to prison culture, the people serving the longest sentences are not the problem, they are the solution. Warden Cain understood this better than most, and when he arrived, he transformed Angola by giving men like Eric a way to channel their determination to atone. In 1995, Angola opened a four-year, accredited seminary operated by the New Orleans Baptist Theological Seminary. The first of its kind in the country, it draws its students from men serving life sentences. Students receive an education in theology, along with classes in math, science, English literature, and history. But as a program intended to create prison ministers, the students also receive training in the skills they most need inside the walls: leadership, counseling, conflict management, grief and trauma support, and peer-to-peer ministry. Warden Cain calls it "moral rehabilitation."[34] Eric was part of the first class, the youngest student in a cohort of eighteen. He received his associate's degree in 1997 and his bachelor's degree in Christian ministry in 1999. From 1996 to 2004, violence at Angola fell by 90 percent, which Cain attributes to the work of prison ministers like Eric.

For Eric, the seminary began a long, transformative process. It gave him an opportunity to make good on his commitment to the single juror who he thought had saved his life, as well as his parents who visited Eric every month and were a constant presence and connection to a life outside of prison. Eric has been a mentor and minister to hundreds of men in Louisiana prisons. But much more than that, in learning how to mentor and comfort other men who were hurting, Eric finally came to understand his own trauma. It is wrong to call the work he did in seminary and afterward a form of therapy—as the abolitionist Andrea Ritchie once said to me, no one goes to therapy in a cage—but Eric's time in seminary helped him begin to understand why he was always angry and ashamed, why the switch was always on, and why he had sometimes exploded so irrationally. It awakened in him a desire to understand how people react to and recover from trauma and abuse, and to help them in their journey. And it enabled him finally to turn the switch off by having some compassion for himself and for those who hurt him so badly as a child.

Service has become Eric's life work. He spent years as an inmate minister, counseling men in prisons throughout the Department of Corrections. Since 2015, he has been a mentor in an innovative reentry program that would've been unthinkable when he was convicted in the early 1990s. Louisiana has created a number of reentry courts. Defendants sent to Angola from a reentry court are housed in a separate unit of the prison, where they receive vocational training and intensive rehabilitative counseling. If they successfully complete the two-year program, they are released early; if not, they are dismissed from the program and placed in the general population to serve their full sentence.

But who provides this counseling and who decides if they have successfully completed the program? Who decides if they are serious in their determination to change, or if they are just trying to game the system in order to avoid many long years at Angola? If they stumble along the way, who decides if their transgressions are serious enough to warrant their dismissal from the program? These decisions are made by mentors like Eric, who not only administer the program and run the classes; they also advise the court on whether a person is a successful candidate for early release. All the mentors are serving life sentences, which means the Louisiana Department of Corrections trusts them enough to prepare men for a productive life in the free world but not enough to live that life themselves. It trusts the mentors enough to decide when a man should be free but not enough to be free.

Eric's current lawyer has assembled letters from some of the men whose lives have been touched by his mentorship. Page after page of testimonials attest: "Eric played a crucial role in helping me to make the changes that I desperately needed to make.... Though our backgrounds are different, we connected. He understood the humanity in others and was able to gracefully encourage guys, myself included, that life beyond all the gates and bars was worth fighting for. It seems crazy that a man who only dreams of life outside of prison encourages and fights for guys who will be released in a matter of months.... His attitude really influenced my drive to make changes in my own life." Another says, "He has become the only person that I turn to when times get tuff. Any time I come to him he always has soft words of wisdom for me. There has even come a time when I needed Eric's advise [*sic*] on an important matter, he calmly got up out of his sleep and like always gave me the kind words that I needed." Testimonials show he has "changed lives in the prison, equipped guys with tools to make a good honest living upon release, and to do these things just because they are the right thing to do." Still another person writes, "I've always marveled at his patience dealing with difficult people. Countless times, I've observed Eric nurture healthy and safe relationships with men, young and old, necessary for continued growth." Another says Eric "inspired me to not only join the New Orleans Baptist Theological Seminary, but to complete it with earning an Associate and Bachelor's Degree in Christian Ministry."

I saw for myself Eric's effect on people. During one of my first visits, a young man rushed up to him—he looked to me no older than twenty—and said, "Eric! I want you to meet my mom," gesturing to the woman standing next to him. "Mom, this is the guy I been telling you about. This is Eric." Eric extended his hand, which the woman took and held for a long time. Looking intently into Eric's eyes, she said simply, "Thank you. *Thank* you. *Thank. You.*" Eric muttered awkwardly about not being the one who did all the work, then added, "Well, I'm a hugger, so if you're ok with it..." The woman gladly accepted the invitation, and the two embraced for a long time. When I saw Eric a few months later, he told me the young man had successfully completed the program and been released. His mother was thanking Eric for returning her son.

Because there are so many letters about Eric's mentorship from so many men, they risk blurring together. Then we recall that each represents a separate life changed by a man who killed an innocent child:

> I have nothing now to hide from any man, woman, or child and therefore say what I know to be correct from deep in my soul: I find that Eric Matthews is one of the most sincere, most remorseful, most understanding, most appreciative inmate that I have ever come across in this penitentiary, which I have been incarcerated for over 30 years now!

4.

There are a lot of statistics in this chapter, but this one might be the most eye-popping: If you added up all the people in every state and federal prison in the country in 1970, the total would still be smaller than the number of people serving a life sentence in 2020. Though the total number of life sentences has declined slightly since then, there are still nearly 200,000 people in the United States who have been sentenced to life imprisonment. That's one out of every six prisoners.[35]

As of 2024, about 5,500 of those people were doing their time in Louisiana. Louisiana isn't the state with the most people serving life sentences; that distinction belongs to California. In fact, in eight states there are more people serving life than there are in Louisiana, though they are all substantially larger states. And Louisiana doesn't have the highest percentage of its prisoners serving life. That too would be California, where nearly four in ten prisoners are serving a life sentence. But in California, the great majority of lifers have at least the possibility of parole. Not so in Louisiana, where more than 95 percent of the lifers have been sentenced either to life without the possibility of parole, or to a sentence longer than fifty years, what researchers call de facto or virtual life. This is a much higher percentage than in nearly any other state. And in Louisiana, nearly three in four lifers are Black. It's this combination that makes Louisiana unique.

Mississippi is similar, but the disparities are not as stark and the total number of lifers is much smaller. In Louisiana more than anywhere else, it is Black men who are sentenced to die in prison.[36]

The unforgiving society protests that most people serving a life sentence have committed murder, and that they must pay with their freedom. But this is no response. For decades, prisoners in Louisiana served ten years and six months for murder.[37] In practice, that's what a life sentence meant in Louisiana. Prison terms did not begin to ratchet up until the 1970s, as suburbanization and ghettoization transformed New Orleans and turned places like St. Thomas into killing fields. The same Louisiana Constitution of 1974 that gutted the city's power to levy property taxes ended the automatic parole that took place after ten years and six months, and in 1979, the Louisiana legislature repealed the 10–6 law. What's worse, they made the repeal retroactive, which dashed the hopes of anyone serving a life sentence at the time.[38] Other states followed a similar pattern. Life sentences began to increase nationwide in the 1970s and '80s, just as the parallel processes of suburbanization and ghettoization were gutting major cities and creating places like St. Thomas all over the country. Yes, three decades ago, Eric Matthews took an innocent life. And every day since then, he has paid a price and tried to atone. The forgiving society asks finally: How much is enough?

5.

Eric's days blend together. He lives in a large, crowded barracks reserved for men in the reentry program. Fifteen bunk beds line the left wall, fifteen more line the right. Down the middle, there are two rows of thirteen cots. When it's full, and it nearly always is, eighty-six men live in the dorm. Eric sleeps on the top bunk in the farthest corner, so that if he turns at night, he can see the wall of the dorm rather than the dozens of men for whom he is responsible. The days start early. The first meeting is at six thirty, followed by a day full of classes. But as busy as he is, the memory of what he did never leaves him. "There's no recovery from that," he told me during one visit.

He rises long before dawn in the hope that he might steal a few moments for himself. But there are always men who wake up even earlier or who never slept at all, and who need to talk. They buttonhole Eric, pulling him aside to seek his calm reassurance or wise counsel. Cohorts of men come to the unit. They begin their passage through the reentry program. Eric and his fellow mentors coach them to become the person they always could have been, to shed the habits of mind that served them so poorly for so long and that landed them in Angola: the anger, the shame, the self-loathing. They graduate and return to society. As one leaves, another soon takes his place. "They all start with me for the first ninety days."

That's where I thought this chapter would end. Instead, Eric got very lucky. In 2021, a lawyer in New Orleans agreed to represent him pro bono. In 2023, she filed a petition for post-conviction relief, arguing that Eric's lawyer at trial had been ineffective. Normally, these petitions have to be filed within two years of when a defendant's initial appeals are over, and Eric's petition was long out of time. But he got lucky again when the prosecutor assigned to the case waived the time limits. The prosecutor's boss later tried to claw back that waiver, but the courts wouldn't permit it, and on July 1, 2024, the district court set aside his conviction and granted him a new trial. He was released the same day, after more than thirty years in custody. (The Louisiana legislature later changed the rules to forbid prosecutors from waiving these time limits. The prosecutor who waived them in Eric's case resigned from the office.)

But that was not the end of the matter. A new set of prosecutors promptly recharged Eric with murder and vowed that they would send him back to Angola for the rest of his life. But Eric got lucky a third time and was assigned two very talented lawyers from the Orleans Parish public defender, who defended him aggressively. In the end, the prosecutors relented and allowed Eric to plead guilty to a reduced charge of manslaughter. On August 15, 2025, the court sentenced him to thirty years in prison but gave him credit for the thirty years he had already served. And with that, Eric Matthews was a free man. He now lives and works in New Orleans.

CHAPTER 3

"WHAT THE FUCK IS WRONG WITH THIS KID?"

> Dzierson picked up Morgan . . . and drove him to Cook's house [where] Cook and Whaley were waiting, and Whaley, armed with a large stick, greeted Morgan by hitting his kneecaps. From there, Morgan was beaten, cut and bound, had salt rubbed into his cuts, was eventually killed—strangled—and had bleach poured down his throat.
>
> —JOSEPH MAHER, "Cook, Whaley Sentenced for Murder—Judge Says Both Men 'Lucked Out' Because of Age," *Schenectady Gazette*, February 23, 1999

1.

To survive the box, you learn to fish. People on the outside call it solitary confinement, but it isn't really, not even at a place like Upstate Correctional Facility, the supermax prison in Malone, New York, ten minutes from the Canadian border. It's true at Upstate you're locked down twenty-four hours a day. It's true you spend twenty-three of those hours in a small concrete and steel cage, and that the twenty-fourth hour is spent in another concrete and steel cage that's connected to, but even smaller than, the first. It's true that for the whole time you're at Upstate, you might not touch another human being, and it's true you won't see another person except through a tight mesh of steel wire and reinforced glass. And it's true you might be locked down for years.

But man is a social animal, and even in a place like Upstate, people will find a way to communicate. They will always buy, sell, and barter stuff, they will always shout to be heard, they will always exchange ideas and create community, and most of all, they will always frustrate the facility's insistence that they be alone. The New York Department of Corrections calls it "secure housing," the outside world calls it solitary, but to the people inside it's just the box. Social and economic life goes on in every box in every New York prison, and the string that holds it all together is fishing.

"So, there's a space underneath the door about yea big." Lucas Whaley held his index finger and thumb about an inch apart. "And you'll take a toothpaste tube and squish it flat. You know, like half used ones but flat, and you'll poke a hole through the back of it and unwind some string from your blanket and tie it through that hole and then attach whatever you're gonna attach to it, and you.... Like, guys are really good at it. They can like, bank it off the wall across the cell to get it down. And then, you'll call down if it doesn't reach the guy. 'Hey, anybody see that line? Can you send that down to whatever cell?' And this is how things move back and forth. That is fishing."

Anything you can attach to a string, you can fish. Food. Tobacco. Rolling paper. Porn. It all gets slid under, passed through, or tossed between the bars of New York State's prisons. But you can also fish an ideology. You can send the banned books that have been surreptitiously passed for decades. The administration seizes these books when they find them, but another copy will soon arrive, smuggled in by inmates or carried in by correctional officers. You can find them in every prison in the country. They're the sacred texts of prison gangs, studied and debated with a reverence that would be familiar to any religious scholar.

"Every organization has like a list of books that they would push and like, it was required reading," Lucas said. Everything was laid out, "almost like a syllabus. They're like, 'you have to read this here. Read this next. Read that next.' It was your education, and really, it just radicalized the fuck out of everybody because it was radical stuff." Radical, but also deadly serious. "People would be pissed if you got given this book and you still haven't read it," he said. "People would get upset like really, really angry with you. You become a conversation in the group, like, 'Listen, man, you need to start like studying. Like, be more serious about it.' It was serious shit."

If there's one place where gangs don't have to worry about their literature getting read, it's in the box. In New York prisons, the first week in the box is a special kind of torment. No reading material of any kind. No radio. No music. No pictures of family. No personal property. No paper. No pen. Nothing but a cell about the size of a parking space. Concrete floor and ceiling. Steel bed, steel toilet, steel chair, and steel sink, all of which are bolted to the wall.[1] One blanket, one sheet, and a two-inch thick mattress. When you're locked down, especially in the beginning, you'll read *anything*. If somebody fishes you something to read, you don't just read it. You devour it.

And it's not just the boredom, which is hell. A lot of people inside have told me that the most dangerous place in any prison is their cell. The first time someone who had spent decades in prison told me that, I didn't understand. I thought he was talking about being attacked by his cellmate, and I muttered something about a single cell being safer. "No!" he said. "That's even worse." He explained that for a lot of guys, the worst times come when they're alone with their thoughts. When you're out of your cell, there's always something that keeps your attention. A correctional officer is hollering at you or somebody else. A fight is about to break out. "There's always drama," Lucas told me. You have to be hyper-attuned to the infinite number of rules and risks that come with living in prison, which means there's always *something* to occupy your mind, and anything is better than being locked inside your head.

Lucas said when he first got to prison, he went looking for trouble. And why not? He was seventeen when he was arrested and eighteen when a judge sentenced him to twenty-five years to life. If he was lucky, he'd be out after a quarter century, but that might as well be life for an eighteen-year-old. "The only thing that helps you escape from something that's that big is something that's more immediate. And so, you know, I did things to put myself in dangerous situations to avoid thinking about doing twenty-five to life." He got into a lot of fights, smoked a ton of weed, and drank as much alcohol as he could get his hands on, which is pretty much what he had been doing in the years before he got locked up. "The action gives you something else more immediate to focus on. You never have to think about what's going on with you." He was also scared shitless. "I was like 160 pounds soaking wet. I was so young. I have pictures still from those years and I was a little guy. I was from a town that nobody had ever heard of. I didn't belong to any gang. It was tough, and it was scary." So, he could either cower in the corner, which is the surest way in prison to become a victim, or he could punch somebody in the face.

Before he was shipped to Upstate, Lucas had been at Coxsackie Correctional Facility, an especially violent prison in Central New York. ("Five kids died in my first summer there," Lucas said. "They used to keep an ambulance on standby in the truck trap when we would go to the yard.") Because Lucas had strangled a man to death, the administrators at Upstate put him in a cell by himself. So, there he was, alone with his thoughts and nobody to punch. By this time, he was nineteen. When they first put him in the box, he was relieved to discover it was freezing and filthy, which meant he could get pissed at the guards for putting him in a hell hole, and that he could spend a couple hours cleaning it, using part of his tiny allotment of toilet paper. Anything to keep his mind occupied. But you can only clean a prison cell with toilet paper for so long, and when he was finally done, his head was waiting for him—the people he beat up, the relationships he destroyed, the opportunities he wasted, the life he took. When his mind finally came to rest, the voice in his head resumed its familiar refrain. "Whaley, you're a colossal fuck-up. Your step-dad was right. You're such a fucking waste. You're gonna die here and that's exactly what you deserve."

And then the skinheads fished him an escape.

2.

Nearly all the recruitment literature of white supremacy slid to a stop in front of Lucas's cell. *Deceived, Damned, and Defiant*, the collected writings of white supremacist David Lane, who coined the infamous 14 words, one of the most important sentences in white supremacist ideology: "We must secure the existence of our people and a future for white children." Lane was convicted and sentenced to 190 years in connection with the murder of Alan Berg, a Jewish radio host in Colorado. In prison, he drafted his *White Genocide Manifesto*, proclaiming that "all Western nations are ruled by a Zionist conspiracy to mix, overrun and exterminate the White race," and calling on all true Aryans to rise up and resist "the Zionist destroyer."[2] *Creed of Iron*, by Lane's protégé, Ron McVan, included apocalyptic exhortations to defend WOTAN, the Will of the Aryan Nation. As McVan saw the world, Aryans are responsible for all the greatest achievements in Western civilization, yet "Aryan man must now face the very real prospect of total race extinction. Every second of every day the future for our children dwindles before our eyes in the stepped up, relentless onslaught of forced integration, immigration and miscegenation. Whether we like it or not, we are living under the dictates of a tyrannical, anti-White 'One World Government' whose interests are in complete opposition to the welfare of our kind."[3] *The White Man's Bible*, by Ben Klassen, revealed "the awesome power of Jewish money and how it has enabled this perfidious race to capture the government, the news media and every other nerve center of power." As Klassen saw it, Jews use their "treacherous deceptions... to mongrelize us, the White Race, in order to force-feed and pump the black blood into the veins of White America."[4]

The literature arrived at a moment when Lucas was "just really susceptible to this kind of thinking." He thought back on his time at Coxsackie. "There were a lot of fights that I had that were started simply because I was white or somebody thought they could take advantage of me because I was white or they didn't like me because I was white." The literature gave him a new language for an old anger. Yet even then, Lucas knew the fights and racial conflict he'd had were not the most important thing in his turn to white supremacy.

Slightly more important was the message that has seduced countless young men since time immemorial: Become part of something bigger than himself, something noble and pure. Be welcomed into a band of courageous warriors, all of them steeling themselves for the battles to come. "We were *so* against drugs. Like, 'you have to quit smoking, no drug use. Nobody drinks.' Everybody was like, you know, 'you got to have a clear head.' Strong mind, strong body, that was what we used to say. Strong mind, strong body." The literature of white supremacy promises what so many young men have always sought: the chance to become the hero. Different causes appeal to different people, but it is no coincidence that, if you swap out the proper nouns, the recruitment pitch to join ISIS sounds a lot like the recruitment pitch to join the Aryan Brotherhood.[5] The imagined nobility of it all has lured countless people into extremism, especially young men, and while it appealed to Lucas as well, this too only took him so far. "I had already read *Mein Kampf* by this time and pretty much concluded that Hitler was a clown."

Even more important than being a noble race warrior was the sense of absolution that white supremacy supplied. As Lucas said, "Being racist is like having a superpower in a way. It feels empowering, because you don't have to like, take the blame for any of your problems. All of your problems are because of someone else. You were born absolutely awesome. You were born superior to everybody else. Everything that's wrong is somebody else's fault. I'm awesome. Fuck these guys. 'Yeah, you're fucking right. God damn, this is everybody else's fault. Fuck these guys.' That's how it felt. It felt like absolution. Like, 'oh, I'm not to blame for any of this.'" For Lucas, white supremacy had the glorious ability to make the voice in his head shut the fuck up.

Yet there was still one thing that had an even more potent effect than absolution. White supremacy welcomed his rage, and that made it irresistible.

3.

Lucas grew up in Johnstown, New York, a small town an hour west of Albany. Johnstown and neighboring Gloversville were once the center of the American glove industry. Legend has it that, at the start of the twentieth century, there were more millionaires per capita in Gloversville than anywhere else in the country. Scores of factories and lots of work. Times were good, until the '70s and '80s, when industry raced out of the United States as if the air had been poisoned. Johnstown became a slump-shouldered used-to-be that limped from food pantry to church basement to tavern, a warren of dead tanneries, empty homes, and overgrown lots.[6]

Lucas's father left when he was an infant, and Lucas has only seen him a couple of times in his life. As a child, Lucas was small and skinny. He kept to himself and didn't have a lot of friends. But he had his books, his imagination, and his mother, and that was always enough. He fell in love with books even before he could read and spent hours flipping through the pages of his mother's collection of science fiction and fantasy. Lucas stared in wonder at the pictures of strange creatures and make-believe worlds. She read to him from an early age and nourished his budding love of fantasy. "I always thought my kids would be geeks," she told him years later. Lucas learned to read when he was very young and devoured the comic books his mother bought him. Later, she got him a set of Legos, and that became his happy place: a geeky little boy, playing with his Legos, reading his comics, and dreaming of other worlds. His pillowcase had images of British colonial soldiers on it, and as he drifted off to sleep, he thought the heartbeat in his ear was the sound of the soldiers on his pillow marching across a field.

Times were good when Lucas was little, until suddenly they weren't. When Lucas was very young, his mother took up with Joe, a biker who made his living selling drugs and made Lucas's life a living hell. Joe was everything Lucas wasn't. He was oversized and loud, and looked at books the way a cow might look at leather shoes if he knew how they were made. Everything about Lucas seemed to piss Joe off. He was too little. Too nerdy. Too lost in his damn comic books. "He used to beat the shit out of me," Lucas said. And as bad as the violence was, the ridicule was worse. Joe seemed to take special pleasure in making Lucas miserable. Whatever Lucas enjoyed, Joe mocked. Whatever he was good at, Joe ridiculed. Comic books were for sissies. Legos were for pussies. The only time Lucas was safe was after Joe had gone to bed.

He and his mother had been so happy. They had their books. They had their fantasy worlds. They had each other. But then she brought Joe into their life. He was bad enough, but his mother had let it happen. She didn't stop the beatings or prevent the ridicule.

She didn't protect him. Lucas didn't know words like *abandoned*, *betrayed*, or *helpless*, but he knew how he felt. "I just remember being really unhappy and sad," he told me. "All the time." When children are mistreated by someone close to them, the deepest scar is generally the one they carve into their own psyche. Like many abused children, Lucas blamed himself for the suffering he endured, reasoning that if he was bludgeoned by someone who should love and protect him, it must be because he was unworthy of love and protection. Perversely, the worse the beatings became and the longer his mother allowed them to go on, the more he despised himself, for only someone truly undeserving would be allowed to suffer such misery.

To be so sad and so young, without either the words to describe the pain or a protector to make it stop, produced an agony that Lucas could not endure. And so it was that he found himself alone in his room, with a ball of yarn and a plan. He unfurled the yarn, coiled it around his neck, tied the other end around a hook in the wall that held up the curtains, climbed onto a chair, and stepped off. He was six. "I remember I was choking. I started to see tunnel vision." Lucas would've killed himself that day, "but in the end the hook bent and the yarn slipped off." It would be years before he told anyone what he had done. By that time, he was already in prison for murder.

A child in this kind of pain will do what they can to make it stop. But Lucas had no outlet for his sadness and no words for his self-loathing. As C. S. Lewis wrote many years ago, "it is easier to say 'My tooth is aching' than to say 'My heart is broken.'"[7] For Lucas, as for many abused boys, the easiest way to escape his torment was to get angry—to have something in front of him that he could scream at until he lost his voice. Something he could punch and rip and scratch and break until he collapsed in exhaustion.

He could get angry at his stepfather, and he did. He could kick and yell, and even though Joe beat him senseless, he eventually looked forward to their fights because it gave him more reason to be angry, which was so much better than being sad. But there was something else, too, something even stronger. Lucas once told me that rage was his superpower. When he was furious and destroying everything he could get his hands on, "it was the only time I felt powerful." For a little boy who was helpless and consumed by self-loathing, this sense of power was intoxicating. "It *filled* me," he said. Growing up, he contrived reasons to be angry and excuses to be violent. He fought all the time, and after every fight, "win, lose or draw, I felt this sense of release. It felt great, and I wanted to feel that way again." In this way, Lucas discovered the addictive power of fury: Like a designer drug, it makes you feel invincible, and like crack, you'll sell your grandmother's soul to get more.

By the time he was fourteen, he was living on his own; he spent much of the next three years breaking shit. He was belligerent and defiant, doing everything he could to cultivate the image of a delinquent hell-raiser. He lived in the basement apartment of a house owned by his grandmother, but he didn't spend much time there. On most nights, he'd be roaming the streets, looking for a building to deface, a window to break, a party to crash, a face to punch. I asked him to tell me what a typical day looked like. He said, "There really isn't much to tell. It was just partying, hanging out, causing trouble, getting in fights." The days blurred together, fueled by mountains of alcohol and weed. He'd "wake up, start drinking, hang out, watch old fucking black and white movies, maybe read, then just start calling around, find out where the party is, go to parties, start fights."

At the time, he said the way he was living didn't feel like pointless nihilism, but it sure sounded that way to me. Then he asked if I had seen the movie *Dark Knight Returns.* "There's this great scene between Christian Bale [Bruce Wayne] and Michael Caine [his butler, Alfred Pennyworth]." Describing the Joker, Bruce says, "criminals aren't complicated, Alfred. We just have to figure out what he's after." Alfred answers with a story about his days in Burma, searching unsuccessfully for a bandit who was stealing gems. "One day, I saw a child playing with a ruby the size of a tangerine. The bandit had been throwing them away." Bruce looks at Alfred, perplexed. "So why steal them?" he asks. "Well, because he thought it was good sport. Because some men aren't looking for anything logical, like money. They can't be bought, bullied, reasoned or negotiated with. Some men just want to watch the world burn."[8]

The movie didn't come out until Lucas was in prison, but when he saw it, he recognized himself. "That scene resonated so deeply with me. I saw myself as a teenager in that sentiment." Like the Joker, Lucas wanted to be the anti-hero, the rebel who could not be bought, bullied, or reasoned with. He told me he had "an inchoate revolutionary stance to, like, destroy the system I hated, to be the bad guy.... There were no end goals. It was just about causing damage. It was just about releasing anger on society, on people."

When he was sixteen, the police pulled his fingerprint off a pistol and charged him with attempted possession of a firearm. He served six months in the county jail and was shocked by the sadistic brutality he saw on the inside, from guards beating handcuffed prisoners, to prisoners beating defenseless inmates while guards stood by. "I saw a kid forced to rape himself with a deodorant bottle." When he got out of jail, he was seventeen and more committed than ever to senseless violence. I asked him how he thought all this would end. "I didn't," he said. "I didn't think about it."

There are thousands of murders in the US every year, but only a few make the national news. The murder of John Morgan in 1998 was one that did. He'd run up a big phone bill and tried to put it in someone else's name, and he'd stirred up a bunch of shit that got a lot of other people in trouble. There was also talk that he was planning on skipping town and leaving everyone in the lurch. He was nineteen.

"So, the plan was to lure him out of his house, to kidnap him, and bring him back to Ted's house," Lucas said. "That, we did pretty easily. Amanda knocked on the door, he came out to talk to Amanda, I grabbed him, threw him in the car, and we brought him back to Ted's house." To the extent the plan had a part B, Lucas said they wanted to "make an example of him for trying to avoid his debts." But that quickly spiraled out of control, and before it was over, Lucas and his codefendants had tied Morgan up in the basement, cut and beat him severely, poured salt in his wounds, and strangled him with an extension cord. After he was dead, Lucas poured a bottle of bleach down his throat.

By the time he got to prison, violent rage was Lucas Whaley's drug of choice, and white supremacy told him that this addiction was a good thing. In fact, it was *exactly* what his people needed. White supremacy scoffed at the memory of all those limp-wrist counselors who had droned on about how he needed to control his anger. They had it backward! The white race needed Lucas to get mad and stay mad—at the Blacks and the Jews and the Mexicans and the Muslims. At everyone but himself. Violence and rage were not the problem, they were the solution. Lucas was instantly hooked.

4.

Lucas spent four months at Upstate, and by the time he was shipped to Great Meadow Correctional Facility in Comstock, New York ("everybody in prison just calls it Comstock"), he had the unmistakable zeal of a white supremacist convert. "Oh yeah. Goose-stepping across the yard. Playing the craziest like, white nationalist music like, at the top [volume] of the radio. Just like, out of control, *all* the time." He spent sixteen months at Comstock but said he was surprised he lasted that long. "I got in a *lot* of trouble. Of the sixteen months I was there, I probably did eleven of it on keeplock, easy." (Keeplock is one step down from the box. Lucas said, "In keeplock, they're just, like, 'you can't come out of your cell.' All your meals get delivered; you're not going anywhere.") But when he wasn't in his cell, he was making trouble. Even in a maximum-security prison, Lucas stood out. "I was stirring shit up and like, it was causing all kinds of tension and violence all across the jail.... People were like, 'What the fuck is wrong with this kid?'"

White supremacists believe that a race war is inevitable,[9] and Lucas spent much of his time at Comstock getting ready. "Everybody is convinced like, there's gonna be a huge race war and it's important that we're ready to fight it, and that we win, and that everybody else would be gone and there'd only be white people left, and like, this is how it's gonna go." Lucas never doubted that war was coming. "I was preparing for a war in the facility. I figured that it would happen around the world and when it [did], it would be, like, happening in prison for sure. I definitely had my doubts about anybody surviving," he said, but he figured that if he was going to die in the war for whiteness, he "wanted to make sure that, like, I sold my life as dearly as possible." He got a vocational job in the welding shop because he could smuggle out welding rods and stash them in the yard. Comstock is an old facility, and the concrete in the yard is cracked and broken. "We just used to take chunks of concrete up [and shove] sharpened welding rods down there. We had *so* many knives, it was a ridiculous amount. We probably could've thrown them at people and still had one for each hand."

Yet as much time as Lucas spent stashing weapons, he spent even more recruiting new members. Recruiting came easy to him, in part because prisons are intensely racialized spaces. Even more than in the free world, many people inside see the world in black and white, and it's easy to interpret conflict in prison through a racial lens. Still, not every white supremacist could have sold white supremacy as successfully as Lucas. He is not a joiner, and though he considered himself a white nationalist, he never became a formal member of any gang. Instead, ever the bookworm, he read and mastered the literature of every gang, even the Black nationalists, which gave him a unique ability to speak everyone's language. At the same time, his addiction to rage and appetite for violence meant he was always eager to lead from the front, and he was more than happy to start any fight that needed to be fought. This combination of leadership and learning quickly made an impression, and before long, the various white supremacist groups at Comstock had set aside their differences and united behind him, "and then slowly I became like the guy in charge." Prison culture is exquisitely sensitive to power, and the respect Lucas commanded made him ideally suited to bring new recruits into the fold. Soon, it was Lucas who was sliding *The White Man's Bible* under the door of someone's cell.

But as important as it was for the white supremacists to recruit members and stash weapons, it was far more urgent to create a sense of shared purpose. "There's always community building going on in prison," Lucas told me. "All the time. That's always happening." For the white supremacists at Comstock, that meant gathering during "night yard," from 7 to 10 p.m. "On a typical night, there's probably about eighty guys there," he said. "We had the handball courts all the way in the back. We'd head out there, say hello to everybody...see everybody, say 'what's up?' and that's like a big deal. [If] people don't see you for a little while, they wonder what's going on. So, you got to go out there and say hello to everybody."

And after checking in, the meeting became part classroom, part ideological proving ground. "It was just talking about things that we had read over the course of the day....What we thought about it, how we were applying it to things that we saw in the news or in our lives, and very often there would be like, debates about like, what certain things meant. Other books would come up, [and] how it relates to other ideas." Always, events were interpreted through the infallible lens of white supremacy. How does that relate to what David Lane had written? What would Ron McVan have said about this? To Lucas, the debates felt urgent and vital. "At the time, I thought I was on the cutting edge of something really important." The rituals and rhythms of night yard enabled the white supremacists at Comstock to forge their identity and become the ideologically pure army needed for the war ahead.

Lucas got into more than his share of fights at Comstock, but he also discovered one of the great paradoxes of prison life: The more he was willing to be ruthlessly violent, the safer he became. Plus, Lucas had one advantage that many prisoners do not. Prison makes life harder in just about every respect, but at least in New York State, there is a white supremacist exception to the rule. "I got rewarded for it. All the time." Whenever Lucas got in trouble, one officer in particular would rally to his defense. "He would come specifically, no matter where he was working in the jail, and come and take me to my ticket hearing and talk to the lieutenant and try to like, get me mercy. He was all about what I was doing." The officer who worked in the package room was also a friend to the cause. He opened every package mailed to Lucas and his associates, but rather than seize the white supremacist literature, he let it all in. "He was like, congratulating guys when they got that kind of knowledge. We were getting stuff in that there was no way we were supposed to be getting." The civilian in charge of the welding shop was another ally. He "was *really*, *really* good to me.... He was always, like, 'attaboy.' So, I got a lot of like, positive reinforcement from the stuff that I was doing. From civilians, from guards, from guys on the outside."

Lucas could've spent his entire prison bid organizing white supremacists behind his leadership, but given the "shit" he was "stirring up," it was probably just a matter of time before major violence erupted. It started when a friend and fellow white supremacist got into a fight. Lucas said, "He knocked out a Muslim kid. Broke his jaw, like, knocked out a bunch of his teeth. He just, he crashed him and dropped the kid." His friend then sought out Lucas for backup, which Lucas was happy to provide. One thing led to another, "and the Muslims are all rolling up on him so we pulled up and then they started fighting and I ran in and things got crazy from there. So, it was a bad, bad fight." Before it was over, about 350 men had joined the brawl. Lucas was lucky. He escaped with nothing more serious than five stitches in his nose. The facility shipped him back to the box, this time at Southport Correctional Facility, a supermax like Upstate. He spent four months at Southport before being transferred to one of the most notorious prisons in the United States: Attica.

That's where all the changes started.

5.

There are only a few prisons in the United States that people can identify by name. Alcatraz, in California, which closed in 1963. Leavenworth, in Kansas, the most famous federal penitentiary. Sing Sing, an hour north of New York City, where Julius and Ethel Rosenberg were executed in 1953. And Attica, in the countryside forty miles east of Buffalo, whose name is forever associated with the deadliest prison uprising in US history.

Wrapped in a towering stone wall thirty feet high, two feet thick, and more than a mile long, Attica was built to intimidate. Until very recently, it had the reputation as the toughest place in the state to do time. It's not the isolation; a lot of prisons in New York are isolated. And it's not the level of security. Attica is a maximum-security prison, not a supermax like Upstate or Southport, where everyone is in the box twenty-four hours a day. It's the culture. Attica was known throughout the system for the brutality and corruption of its correctional officers.

"They let you know as soon as you get there, you're in fucking Attica," Lucas said. "You better watch your step. You don't play games there. They've got the beatdown to a fine art." Attica is divided into five cell blocks. When Lucas was there, Blocks A and C were the most violent. Lucas was in Block C. When new arrivals came to the block, the correctional officers "line everybody up. They've got like all the officers out there in the hallway. Everybody's got their batons out." A squad captain "comes around with a clipboard, and he'll ask you your DIN [department ID number] and why you're in his jail." If you came to Attica from a place like Upstate, he wants to know why you were sent to the box; if you came to Attica after your conviction, he wants to know what you did to get locked up in the first place.

But of course, he already knows the answers to his questions. What he really wants is for everyone else to know why you're in "his jail." He wants you to say it out loud, and then he wants everyone to see what happens next. As soon as someone says they had been in the box for assaulting an officer or a sex crime, "you're getting hit, like immediately." That's when the beatdown starts, usually from several officers at once. "You might not even get to finish saying it, and everybody in that line is going to see it. And you better not react. That's how they do things there."

They say Attica is different now—or at least, that it is less violent—and that it got better after 2018, when the Department of Corrections finished installing nearly two thousand surveillance cameras and one thousand microphones, which make it virtually impossible for correctional officers to beat a prisoner without being observed. Before the cameras, officers would defend the use of force by saying a prisoner had assaulted them or that he had a weapon. For years, inmates insisted that these accusations were ginned up after the fact to justify beatdowns administered by guards for no good reason. Once the cameras were up and running, alleged inmate assaults on staff suddenly declined by nearly 80 percent.[10] But none of those changes helped Lucas, who was long gone from Attica by the time the cameras and microphones arrived.

When he got to Attica, Lucas tried to reestablish the white supremacist community he had built at Comstock but quickly discovered that the other white inmates had different priorities. "It was by and large older Italians, some bikers, and then just some random assorted guys," he said. "Mostly in for like robberies and stuff like that. All those guys were racist, but it wasn't an ideology. It's just the way they viewed the world. Just like, 'deal with your own.'" Lucas tried to persuade them. He made all the arguments and gave all the recruitment pitches, but everything that had worked at Comstock fell on deaf ears in Attica. At Comstock, most of the guys were young, like Lucas. But the guys in Attica were older and had been in the system a long time. They knew how to do time and had no interest in some young kid droning on about a looming race war. "They were racist as fuck, but it wasn't a cause," he said.

There was another difference between Attica and Comstock, something that made people even less receptive to Lucas's arguments. "Most of them were drug addicts of one stripe or another." Heroin was big in Attica, and it's hard to convince somebody to keep a strong mind in a strong body when all they can think about is their next fix. Lucas was still a believer and thought the other whites were not sufficiently pure of body and mind: "I was like, that was really the problem. That was what was really preventing them from seeing what I saw." He still thought a race war was coming and "thought all these guys were just ridiculous. They just didn't see it." But you can only beat your head against a wall for so long, so rather than waste his time arguing with people who didn't want to listen, Lucas returned to his first love: "I really just did more reading."

And what was he reading in the most infamous prison in America? "Lots of stuff," he said. "Fantasy, of course. As always, supremacist literature. I started reading a lot of philosophy around that time, too." But most of all, history. White supremacists like David Lane trace their doctrine to a pre-Christian set of Norse religious beliefs and practices known as Odinism, which they have twisted into "Wotanism," conjuring an *-ism* from the acronym WOTAN, the Will of the Aryan Nation. In an effort to understand Wotanism, Lucas worked his way backward, first to Odinism and then even farther back in time. "Scandinavian history, the Viking Age and cultural stuff. Like, that's what I was digging into deep."

And the deeper he dug, the more surprised he became. "That's when I started to realize, like, wait a second. None of the stuff like we think of as race even existed to these people. At all. Not even close. That was *really* surprising to me because that is *not* the way it had been sold to me." Like many religions, Odinism prescribed a code of personal behavior, but it had nothing to do with whiteness or the supposed supremacy of one race over another. The thought slowly began to dawn on Lucas that, contrary to what he had been led to believe, "whiteness was kind of a newer idea that hadn't always existed." The insight shook him. "It was kind of like the first sort of punch on that very narrow pillar I was standing on."

The first punch but not the last. He said, "At the same time, looking at all the white guys that I'm around, most of them are drug addicts, most of them are saying one thing and doing another, you know, expressing very strong morals that they violated all the time." For example, when the older white guys fell behind on their heroin debt, the dealers would offer to excuse the debt if they attacked another prisoner who was even more behind. And they had to do it publicly, so everyone would see what happens to people who don't pay their debts. But rather than do the deed themselves, they'd pressure a young kid to do it by convincing him he needed to establish his reputation in prison. And just as some white prisoners were behaving disreputably, some Black prisoners were living honest, transparent lives, treating Lucas and everyone else with precisely the sort of dignity and respect that Odinism demanded.

Then there were the conversations he had. There were only a few avowed white supremacists in Attica, but one had been with Lucas at Comstock, and Lucas started to share his doubts with him, explaining that Odinism had nothing to do with whiteness. "He very quickly got disgusted with me and started like, separating himself." Lucas being Lucas, he pressed his case: "Hey, race as we understand it hasn't always existed." But the man didn't want to hear it. "He was really, really bothered by that idea. He just brushed it off, wasn't even something that he was willing to consider. 'That's not true. That's just propaganda. This is how it's always been.'"

Lucas figures the change in his own thinking took about two years. "It was a really slow, gradual process." Months of reading, watching, listening, arguing. Months of reflecting, pondering, reassessing. There was no *eureka!* moment. But finally, he came to the only conclusion that history and reason allowed. All the white supremacist literature he had studied? The worldview he had preached? The people he had recruited and the race war he had prepared for? "It was bullshit."

Lucas spent six years at Attica. By the time he left, he had thoroughly turned his back on white supremacy. In fact, he spent most of the final four years working for an inmate who controlled the very lucrative marijuana trade on the block. (Lucas asked me not to identify this person because he is still inside and Lucas doesn't want to make his life more difficult.) It was a good life, if you can say that about any life in a maximum-security prison. They bribed the correctional officers and made a lot of money. "I was doing a really good bid there," he said. "The last Thanksgiving there we spent like a little over $800 and had alcohol and like a whole layout for Thanksgiving and fed all our guys in the entire block.... It was like that scene in *Goodfellas* where they're like cutting up garlic and like hanging out and drinking wine. That was what my bid was like there the last four years." But nothing good lasts for long in prison, and a misunderstanding led to an argument, an argument led to a fight, and a fight led to a brawl involving more than 150 guys, including Lucas. Before long, he was on his way back to the box at Upstate.

6.

"I went to the box with a goal this time," he said. "I'm not gonna say a goddamn fucking word to a living soul the entire time I'm in the box. I'm gonna just read. I got some big ass fucking books in there and that's what I'm gonna do. And that's what I did. No fishing. No nothing. I did four months in the box to myself." I asked him what he read. He couldn't remember everything, but it included *Poetics* by Aristotle and *Meditations* by Marcus Aurelius. "It was a lot of classic stuff."

Reading was part of his stint in the box but not the most important part. Yes, white supremacy was behind him, but Lucas hadn't been a white supremacist when he came to prison either. He wasn't a white supremacist the day he and his codefendant tortured and killed nineteen-year-old John Morgan. Leaving white supremacy wasn't the same as ending the addiction to violence that had landed him in prison. He still had a lot of work to do, and for that, he needed a push. He'd been in the box about three weeks when a CO said he had visitors. They chained him up and walked him to the visiting area. His two brothers and a younger cousin were there. He hadn't seen them since he got to prison and he wondered why they came. They gave him the news. "I remember not having an immediate reaction outside of just shock. And like, the rest of the visit is kind of a blur. I don't really. . . . I just remember feeling kind of numb. And like, separated from myself. And it didn't really hit me until I got back to my cell." Kim had been killed.

Lucas met Kim when he was thirteen and living on the street after one too many beatings by his stepfather. "She was awesome. Like, it's such a cliché to say that everybody loved her, but really everybody loved her." She was kind, generous, and funny. Everything that Lucas was not. And yet for some reason, she loved Lucas and saw him for more than his rage. They were on-again-off-again for years, but Lucas had been too addicted to mayhem to maintain a healthy relationship. "We would be together for a little while and then like something would happen, I would get in a fight or do something crazy. And she would leave. And then we would bump into each other somewhere or I would get drunk and call her and we would get back together and I would try. And things would fall apart. We'd break up and I go from tailspin to nose dive. And she'd come save me." Somehow, Kim always saw past the failures. "She was the only person in my whole life that believed in me. That really believed in me. And I knew it. And I felt it. Every time we were together." (In order to protect her family's privacy and safety, Lucas asked me not to use Kim's last name).

When Lucas was arrested and charged with murder, Kim had visited him regularly in the county jail. They talked about getting married. Then he was in prison looking at twenty-five to life, and Lucas eventually stopped hearing from her. "I figured she smartened up and realized that I wasn't coming home." Part of him thought it was good that she had moved on and given up on a loser like him. She deserved so much better. But part of him clung to the faint hope that she would always be there for him, somehow, someday. When everything else was absolute shit, there was always Kim—one perfect memory, one precious hope. And then she was gone.

Lucas felt like he was falling backward off a cliff with no bottom. Time was a blur, a haze. For three days, he didn't eat and barely slept. Nothing in his life made sense. "I felt like.... Like it wasn't right. Like it wasn't supposed to happen somehow. Somebody had just done something that changed the way the world was supposed to be. And that the world had jumped its tracks. And I just felt like, there must be something somebody could do to make it right. And I knew there wasn't." By this point in our conversation, Lucas was sobbing uncontrollably. He paused, grabbed a tissue, and wiped his eyes. "I felt like the world would never be right again." All the defiance, all the rage, all the violence suddenly felt hollow and pointless. Somewhere in those fevered, grief-stricken days, "I realized that how I was feeling was exactly how I made John's family feel." In the box at Upstate, the enormity of his crime—the pain he caused and the guilt he felt—struck him as it never had before. "We tortured John and strangled him to death and poured a bottle of bleach down his throat. It's fucking heinous," he told me. "It made me feel terrible about myself. It changed everything."

Though the pain never goes away, grief like this doesn't last forever, and at some point, Lucas caught a glimpse of something in a magazine that made him laugh. "And when I laughed, I realized that I wasn't gonna feel like that forever. And I immediately sat down at the desk and started writing. And I wasn't writing about anything that I was feeling or anything that I was thinking and somehow it was about all of that. And I made a promise to myself that whatever it was that Kim saw in me, I was gonna live up to it. And I just kept writing. When I found out she died, I died. And I came out a different person. Someone committed to being better."

7.

It's tempting to believe that Lucas turned a corner that day and never looked back. But he's too honest with himself for fairy-tale endings. "I wish I could say that," he said. "I really do." For many years, volcanic rage had been essential to his identity. It was how he navigated the world, and though it regularly led him astray and had brought him to prison, it had also steered him clear of the far greater pain that came with confronting his own misery. By the time he got to prison, rage was all he knew. It was an addiction.

Besides, it's hard to convince someone in a maximum-security prison that violence is always a bad idea. People inside understand that violence—or more precisely, the widely recognized willingness to be violent—can help you solve very immediate problems (someone wants to rape you) even as it might cause others (so, you cut him and end up in the box). Lucas left Upstate after four months and got shipped to Auburn Correctional Facility, a maximum-security facility and the oldest continually operating prison in the country. Six days later, he got in a fight that landed him in keeplock for thirty days.

If Lucas was going to make good on his commitment to Kim and honor her memory, he needed to develop a new identity, something that allowed him to relinquish the ingrained habits of a lifetime. The opportunity presented itself shortly after he arrived at Auburn, when someone told him about a college program in the prison—the Cornell Prison Education Program—and said he should take the entrance exam. Lucas had far too little faith in himself to believe he could possibly be a college student, so he resisted for a long time. "In my heart of hearts, I felt like I was just a fucking failure who would fail at everything, all the time." But the guy kept pestering Lucas, so finally he filled out the form and took the exam. "I *just* squeaked in."

His first college course was a fiction class taught by the novelist Edward Hower, who lives in Ithaca. He had to submit ten pages a week, plus another one hundred at the end of the term. The class was perfect for Lucas and he poured everything onto the page. He took two classes the next term. Then three classes the semester after that, and three more every semester from that point on. He signed up for whatever they offered: English literature. Biology. History. Political science. Anthropology. Feminist theory. He read voraciously and wrote religiously. He still got in trouble now and again, but he'd keep up with the reading and the assignments while he was in keeplock. He'd give his work to another guy in the class who would turn it in for him. And he never took a semester off, even taking classes over the summer. Gradually, he stopped getting in trouble. There was no time for all that foolishness.

As a professor at Cornell, I know that the magic of a college education has very little to do with the material students learn in class. Whatever Lucas learned about anthropology or feminist theory was far less important than what he learned about himself. For Lucas, it was no small thing to have his arguments and ideas taken seriously, and to see himself as someone capable of critical thought and careful reasoning at the highest level, as someone who could navigate the world with his mind rather than his fists. And because Lucas thrived in the classroom, because he loved everything about it, he learned that his stepfather had been as wrong as a human being could be.

As he was beginning to see himself as a student and thinker, another change was taking hold. By the time he got to Auburn, Lucas had established his reputation in prison. Not simply as the person who fought a lot but the guy who voluntarily left white supremacy. Usually when a person leaves white supremacy in prison, it's not because they reject the ideology but because they broke the rules and got kicked out. They snitched, for instance. This makes them a pariah throughout the facility; they're cast out by the white supremacists but unaccepted by other prisoners, both because they still hold supremacist views and because they can't be trusted. But Lucas never broke the rules. He left because he concluded the ideology of white supremacy was built on a lie, and he had the learning to back it up. And he read voraciously and absorbed the wisdom of every gang's texts.

This gave Lucas a prized role inside: He was almost universally respected. The Bloods and the Nation of Islam respected that he had voluntarily turned away from white supremacy. White supremacists respected that he never broke the rules, even if they disagreed with his decision. People who weren't in a gang respected that he was a stand-up guy who treated everyone with dignity. Everyone respected his intellect, since he read so widely, and most people admired and respected that he was in college, trying to do something with his life. And everyone had to respect that he had earned his place in the prison by being willing to fight; he wasn't a coward or a punk.

Lucas put this respect to good use. He became the mediator, the trusted voice of reason and restraint, an entirely new identity for him. "I was able to end wars," he said. "Just by talking. And sometimes like beefs that had absolutely nothing to do with me.... Just because I didn't think that they needed to happen and I knew that they were going to, so I would get in the middle of it and act as an intermediary and like it became a thing where sometimes guys would bring stuff to me that had nothing to do with me."

Lucas was seventeen when he tortured and killed John Morgan. When the judge sentenced him to twenty-five years to life, he said Lucas was lucky, because if he'd been eighteen, he could've faced the death penalty. The judge made clear that that would've been just fine with him. "You lucked out," he said, adding that he hoped Lucas didn't get out of prison until he was an old man, if at all. After he was sentenced, Lucas told the judge, "You may not think I deserve to be outside, but someday I will get out. And I'll be different."[11]

He spent nine years at Auburn before being transferred to Cayuga Correctional Facility, a medium-security facility, where he spent another four years and continued to take classes through Cornell's Prison Education Program. That's where he and I met; he was a student in two classes I taught at the facility. He always sat in the front row, engaged and eager. My classes in prison are every bit as rigorous as the classes I teach at Cornell but much less formal, and Lucas and I quickly settled into a routine of harmless, if occasionally profane, banter. He was released on parole in 2023, after twenty-five years in custody. Soon after his release, he enrolled in college to finish his degree. He received credit for most of the classes he took with the Cornell Prison Education Program, which allowed him to graduate with honors in December 2024.

Of all the people I have met who served many years in prison and are now out, Lucas is the one I worry about the most. Not because of his addiction to violence; I think he has a handle on that, though he forthrightly says the temptation to be violent never completely goes away. "It's something I'm always going to have to live with." But violence is not his first impulse anymore, and not his second either. Unlike when he was seventeen, he knows what his addiction is and understands where it came from. And at forty-three, he has a set of intellectual outlets and emotional tools that help him manage his anger—tools he didn't have when he was young.

But Lucas's stepfather did something far worse than hook Lucas on rage. As much with his mocking and ridicule as with his fists, he convinced Lucas that he was worthless—that he was and will always be a failure, and in his darkest moments, the voice that Lucas hears in his head tells him that Joe was right. Yes, he proved Joe wrong in prison, but now that he is out, he has to prove it again. And not just once but nearly every day, because anyone with an Internet connection can discover what Lucas did more than a quarter century ago, and in an unforgiving society, far too many of those people believe the leopard never changes its spots. It's hard to believe in yourself when everyone thinks you're a monster.

To those who do not know him well, Lucas still performs the part of thick-muscled hypermasculinity, and once boasted on social media,

"This morning, I marched 2 miles in a 20 lb. vest and carrying 15 lbs. kettlebells. Never set them down. It was a good reminder that I'm a fucking bad ass." But those who know him better see this for what it is: the mask that hides the geeky little boy under the covers with his comic books. In another post, he wrote, "Batman is serious business around here; if you start that conversation, prepare to be responding for weeks." In his Facebook profile, he describes himself as "Writer. Geek. Poly Punk Rock Pirate."

CHAPTER 4

"THE DISQUIETING COMPLEXITY OF OURSELVES"

> Authorities Friday arrested a woman they allege came to the home of an eight-months-pregnant woman, purportedly to buy a dog, then strangled her and cut the baby from her womb. Authorities found the abducted infant in good health, ending a day of frantic searching.
>
> —MARGARET STAFFORD, "Pregnant Woman Found Slain, Baby Found Safe," *Los Angeles Times*, December 19, 2004

1.

It's always hard to pinpoint beginnings, but Lisa Montgomery's story might start in a bar near the sprawling army base in Fort Riley, Kansas. That's where her parents met. John was stationed at the base and spent his spare time drinking. Judy worked in the bar and was paid to separate servicemen like John from their money. She liked John because he made her job easy. He liked Judy because, as he later put it, she was "available and willing." They drank as often as they could and kept on drinking even after Judy got pregnant with Lisa. Years later, John still remembered the time a waitress jokingly carded Judy's fetus.[1]

Or maybe Lisa's story begins even sooner. John struggled with depression for decades, just like his sister and a number of Lisa's paternal cousins. He treated his depression with drink and would later say he spent the better part of two decades, from 1960 to 1980, drinking "all day, every day," which only made his depression worse. On a good night, he said he could limit himself to a case of beer, but there weren't a lot of good nights. On Judy's side, psychosis hopped from branch to branch of the family tree, and it seemed like every other cousin or half brother was on antipsychotics or had spent time in a mental hospital.

After he was discharged, John spent his days barely employed and his nights drinking. When he and Judy got together, his daughter from a prior marriage, Diane, was two. But John was too depressed and drunk to be much of a father, and Judy was too angry to be much of a mother. She hated Diane. Once, when Diane was five and had committed a five-year-old's transgression, her stepmother stripped her naked, opened the front door, and told Diane she had to leave. Diane was crying and begged her parents to let her stay. Seeing how this terrified Diane, Judy made the ritual a regular part of her parenting. "Judy tortured me by pretending that I was about to be sent away from the family, all of the time. She stripped me naked, packed all of my clothes into a suitcase, and forced me outside onto the stoop of the house. She told me that people were just about to come and take me away. I stood out on the stoop of the house, naked and afraid, many, many times." And Judy treated Lisa, her first born, with as little regard as she did Diane. When she cried, Judy put duct tape over her mouth. If she didn't finish her food, Judy strapped her to her high chair and left her there for hours. She disciplined Lisa by holding her under cold water in the shower. Judy used to brag that Lisa's first full sentence was, "Don't spank me. It hurts."

John and Judy fought all the time. They fought over money. They fought over the men Judy brought to the house. They fought over

Diane and Lisa, who always seemed to get in the way of their drinking and fighting. Before long, John abandoned the family, leaving Judy to raise the girls on her own. Lisa was three, and parenting passed to Diane, who was five. "Judy never cared for Lisa," Diane recalled many years later, "and so I took care of Lisa all of the time." She fed and changed Lisa, dressed her, and protected her from the fighting "as best as a small child can. . . . I loved her like I thought a mother should." After John abandoned the family, Judy invited the Kansas Department of Social Welfare to remove her stepdaughter from the home. Social workers determined that Diane's needs had been "totally ignored by the adults who have charge of her." Diane was taken away two weeks shy of Lisa's fourth birthday.

2.

Judy met her second husband in a bar in Tulsa. Jack Kleiner became Lisa's stepfather when she was five. At the time, there was a bus driver named John Francesco, who drove a bus for the Central Assembly of God ministry. The ministry served children living in the poorest parts of Tulsa, and even decades later, John could still recall the "darkness" that hung over Lisa's home. He said Jack, Lisa's stepfather, was "a hard and harsh man," "strict and overbearing." He could never understand "why Jack was so hard on his wife and children," and remembered Lisa as a "fearful" little girl who "didn't want to do anything or step out of line."

That the driver could summon these details is even more striking when you consider the family never lived anywhere for long. Lisa had fifteen different homes by the time she was twelve. She pinballed from Kansas to Washington, back to Kansas and then to Colorado, back to Kansas, then to Oklahoma, California, and Texas, then back to Oklahoma, back to Texas, back to Oklahoma. But wherever they moved, poverty followed them. In Tulsa, John Francesco said they lived in the "ghetto," a neighborhood "rife with crime, prostitution and drugs." When Lisa lived in Sperry, Oklahoma, her family was poor even by the standards of an impoverished, rural town where the median income was less than half the national average. The elementary school once called Judy because Lisa's shoes were held together with duct tape.

Jack Kleiner was an angry man. His children from his first marriage said living with him meant walking on eggshells, knowing that no matter how hard you tried to be invisible, he was going to beat the shit out of you anyway. He smacked Judy and the children as casually as you might smack a mosquito and beat the children "for nothing at all." He once lifted Lisa's baby sister by the pigtails and beat her with a belt for soiling her pants. He broke a broomstick over Lisa's head. People who knew her growing up described Lisa as a "scared little girl" who "lived in her own little world." She was "afraid of her own shadow" and "flinched" when she thought she was "going to get hit."

But from the beginning, there was something different about Jack's anger. When he really wanted to punish Lisa, when he got drunk and wanted to teach her a lesson, he marched her to the bathroom, forced her to strip off her pants, bent her naked over the tub, and beat her from behind. Even as Lisa got older, Jack continued the ritual, stripping his young stepdaughter naked from the waist down, bending her over the tub and whipping her from behind. Judy and Jack would eventually have three children of their own, two of them boys. Jack never subjected the boys to this abuse.[2]

3.

It started when Lisa was about eleven. Jack came to her bedroom, sometimes at night, sometimes during the day. At first, he fondled her breasts. Lisa had learned long ago what happened if she screamed or fought or ran from Jack, but he let her know again. Before long, Jack started to stroke her genitalia. The rapes began when Lisa was thirteen.

Every few days, he came to her. She could feel his breath and smell the rum. It went on for years. Every week. Every month. Every year.

When adults cannot or will not protect them, children will try to shelter at least a tiny part of their mind from the pain and chaos that surrounds them. They dissociate. There are clinical definitions of dissociation—"a disruption in the integration of consciousness, self-perception, memory, and actions"[3] or "the exclusion from consciousness and the inaccessibility of voluntary recall of mental events"[4]—but at its core, dissociation is a defense mechanism. In periods of intense trauma, the brain releases opioids that dull pain, decrease awareness, and fragment memories. This accounts for the sense that survivors sometimes have of leaving their body during a traumatic event, as if they were watching it rather than experiencing it. Lisa began to dissociate. She couldn't escape, so her mind went someplace else.

Another strategy that children sometimes develop to survive life-threatening violence is appeasement. We see this in kidnap victims and hostages too. For the child being raped, this often means learning to feign enjoyment.[5] Like dissociation, appeasement can rewire a child's brain. Children, like everyone else, respond instinctively to threats: they fight, flee, or freeze. These responses are automatic and involuntary. But in a child who must appease her attacker in order to survive, this instinct can be reprogrammed. Appeasement can become a child's instinctive response to threat, every bit as automatic and involuntary as the impulse to resist or escape. What may appear to the outside world as freely chosen, intentional behavior, may actually be a reflexive response to life-threatening trauma.[6]

The cruel irony of appeasement is that people who discover what's happening can convince themselves it's not a big deal because the victim isn't a victim at all. She's not a defenseless child being raped over and over again by her stepfather forty years her senior. She's just a young girl who likes to have sex. Lisa as a sex-crazed teenager would become a prominent theme of the government's case against her. One of her lawyers counted thirty-seven different occasions when the jury heard that Lisa encouraged her stepfather to rape her, and that even as a child, she had been, in the words of a psychologist for the government, "a willing participant" in the innumerable vaginal, oral, and anal rapes she endured from the age of thirteen.[7]

After the rapes began, Jack moved the family to a remote trailer outside of town. He built a separate bedroom for Lisa, with its own entrance to the outside and no access from the trailer. This made it easier for him to rape Lisa; he said he was teaching her how to be a good wife as he sodomized her. For Lisa, the only saving grace was that the family also used her bedroom to store their liquor, and when Lisa wasn't being raped, she was getting drunk. When Lisa was fifteen, Judy walked in on Jack raping Lisa on the floor of Lisa's bedroom. "He was in her," she recounted later. "He was pumping her."[8] But instead of calling the police or seeking help for her child, she kicked Jack out of the house and held a gun to Lisa's head. Two days later, she welcomed Jack back. Judy eventually divorced Jack, and her lawyer arranged for Judy and Lisa to have a few sessions with a child services worker. Judy told the worker that when Lisa was a child, she had "seduced" Jack, "that it was Lisa's fault that Jack raped her, and that Lisa [had been] trying to steal Jack away from her."[9]

We don't know why Judy behaved as she did. Her father had been brutally abusive and Judy said he raped her. She may have felt a need to normalize her own history. But for whatever reason, she didn't just turn a blind eye as her husband repeatedly raped her child. In time, she decided to profit from what she viewed as Lisa's insatiable promiscuity. When men came to work on the trailer—plumbers, electricians, contractors—Judy paid them in free access to Lisa's underage body. A stream of workmen regularly trooped to Lisa's bedroom, sometimes alone but sometimes in groups. A few of the men put money in Lisa's dresser before they left.

Over the years, plenty of people learned that Jack had raped his minor daughter, and some of them had a professional obligation to do something about it. There was the judge who presided over Judy's divorce from Jack. Judy testified about the rape and said she never told anyone because she didn't want to humiliate the other children. The man Judy took up with immediately after Jack was Richard Boman, the chief of police in Sperry. She told him that Jack had cheated on her with her underage daughter, and though this was a crime in Oklahoma (and every other state in the country), Boman did nothing. When Lisa was sixteen, Judy took her to a doctor, who suggested she alert "legal authorities" about the rapes. But he didn't do it and neither did Judy. With all these people, Judy acted as though she were the victim, not Lisa, who was tagged as a "bad" girl who enjoyed illicit sex.[10]

4.

The survival strategies that kept Lisa alive when she was young—dissociation and appeasement—became the reflexes that led her astray as an adult. When trauma is severe but temporary, dissociation can protect a child's mind. But what happens when trauma surrounds a child's entire existence and lasts for years? An expert would later conclude that Lisa's dissociation, one of the most severe she had ever seen, had become "woven deeply into her personality.... Her dissociation is a completely pervasive part of who she is." Because Lisa lived "in a dissociated state much of the time," she was never quite sure what was real, either in her own body or in the world around her. Memory blurred with fantasy, and life "felt like a movie or a fog or a dream."

Lisa was sixteen when Judy married Richard Boman, the Sperry police chief. Judy promptly paired Lisa with Boman's son, Carl, who was seven years older than Lisa. From the beginning, Carl could tell that "something was wrong" with Lisa. She "was not emotionally present. She was in her own world and distant from everything. Lisa went somewhere else mentally. She just was not present." The couple married when Lisa was seventeen. She was pregnant at eighteen and the mother of four by the age of twenty-two.

As an adult, she was alternately manic and chaotic or withdrawn and depressed. Sometimes she disappeared into her room for days, silent and inconsolable. Then she would suddenly emerge "with a plan or an idea and nothing could stop her." At one point, she thought she would can and preserve vegetables but quickly lost track of what was growing where. Later she decided she wanted to raise farm animals and bought goats, lambs, cows, and chickens but had no capacity to care for them and became overwhelmed. One time, she put a diaper on a goat. On a whim, she once declared that she would homeschool the children and took them out of the public school. But the schoolbooks she found were all for younger children, and she couldn't manage the lessons.

Lisa talked nonstop to anyone or no one, repeating herself and not letting others get a word in. But her talk was just a word salad that made no sense. She rambled about "craft project[s], sheep, wools, lawnmowers, quilts, Judy . . . , and back and forth." People would leave the room while Lisa was talking but she simply continued her bizarre monologue. She talked to strangers as if they were old friends. No description appears more often in the records than this sense of Lisa being physically present but mentally absent. Her father-in-law said she "seemed to be in a world of her own." Her children came up with a nickname to bring Lisa back to the real world when she "tuned out." Instead of calling her "mom," they called her "Martha," just to get her "to tune in to us for a little while." Her youngest daughter Kayla would later recall that her "strongest memory about growing up, as well as one of the saddest parts of my life is the fact that my mom was not present. Mom wasn't able to be either mentally or emotionally present in my life, or in the lives of my brother and sisters. She definitely was with me physically, but that is all."

Lisa often remembered things that never happened, wasn't sure whether she had given birth to her fourth child, and sometimes told people that Judy had kidnapped one of her children, a mysterious fifth child named Sarah. Sometimes Lisa said that Judy had put Sarah up for adoption and she spent hours on the Internet searching for her. Other times, she said Judy was keeping Sarah for herself. Her marriage to Carl didn't last, and Lisa bounced with the children from one place to another. Sometimes she lived with a man for a month or two, then would gather up the kids and move across town, across state, or across the country on a moment's notice. Sometimes the family lived in squalor; sometimes they were homeless. She could barely maintain herself, let alone her children. She frequently went long periods without bathing. A friend from childhood saw her once and was struck by "how bad she looked and how terrible she smelled.... To the point you couldn't stand to be next to her. Her hair was greasy and her clothes were dirty, but she didn't seem to notice." Complex tasks were entirely beyond her; when she worked, she could hold down only the simplest jobs that paid next to nothing. And she was far too mentally ill to manage a household and care for her children. The home was a roach-infested shambles. Unwashed dishes gathered in the sink until they became moldy. Trash littered the floor and piled almost to the ceiling. The children often went hungry and wandered to a neighbor in search of food and a bath.

Yet as mentally ill as she was, Lisa's delusions were not random. By all accounts, she loved her children dearly and desperately wanted to provide them with the loving home she never had. Her identity, confused as it was, depended entirely on being—and being seen as—a good mother, and her failings were a constant source of frustration and sadness. At some deep level, she knew this wasn't the life she wanted or imagined for her and her children, but she had no ability to make it better. Though she could not be the ideal mother, she knew how to *become* a mother. As she would later tell a psychologist, the only thing she felt she was good for was "as a body to create babies." In her illness, only one thing made sense: pregnancy.

And perhaps that's not that hard to understand. Pregnant women are celebrated and protected in American society. Glossy pictures of pregnant women on magazine covers invariably show them beaming with joy and gently cradling their bulging belly. People smile and coo over pregnant women and ask solicitously about morning sickness and due dates. For many people, pregnancy is a socially joyful time. Pregnancy gave Lisa membership in a caring and supportive community. Being pregnant provided her with the one thing that few can live without: a sense of belonging, purpose, and achievement.

But after the birth of her fourth child, Lisa had a tubal ligation. She was still with Carl at the time, and when a doctor had recommended the procedure, Carl thought it was a good idea. Though the records are unclear, Lisa may have agreed to the procedure in the way she agreed to everything that men wanted to do with her body. The ligation not only ended her chance for future pregnancies; it severed her abruptly from a social context that showered her with unconditional love and support. Worse, it threatened her identity as someone who could be, and could become, a mother. Even in women who have not been physically and sexually assaulted for years, the sudden realization that they can no longer get pregnant can be deeply traumatizing, and for Lisa, the rupture proved too much.

Something in Lisa's mind repeatedly began to tell her, and she began to believe and to tell the world, that she was pregnant. In time, she would discover she had lost the baby for one reason or another, which threw her deeper into depression. But soon, she would find herself pregnant again, reliving that brief period of joy and excitement, only to see it end in another miscarriage. Pregnancy was her recurring delusion.

Lisa fantasized about reversing her tubal ligation. Sometimes, she was convinced that she had already reversed the procedure. She became obsessed with a cousin, Wendy Treibs, who had two children after her ligation had been reversed. Lisa would eventually describe Wendy as "the perfect mom." She began to dress like Wendy and wear her hair the same way. But Lisa did not have the resources or support to reverse her ligation, and pregnancy remained a fantasy. Yet it was an increasingly urgent fantasy. Her delusions that she was pregnant came with increasing frequency.

In 1994, long after she split from Carl, she told people she was pregnant with twins and bought a crib. She was dating a man who knew nothing of her tubal ligation, and he believed she was pregnant. But when Judy confronted her, she reported vaguely that she had had a miscarriage. In 1999, she said she was pregnant again; her partner at the time opposed childbirth out of wedlock, and Lisa told him she traveled to Nevada for an abortion. Six months later, she said she was pregnant again. She claimed to end this pregnancy by drinking a concoction of pennyroyal leaves.

In late 2001, she said she became pregnant a fourth time. By this time, she had remarried and was so convinced she was pregnant, and so convincing, that her husband Kevin thought "her breasts were larger and tender, her belly got bigger, and her periods stopped." Kevin pressed her to go to the doctor for prenatal care, and when she finally did, she said the fetus "had complications with blood and that her body was rejecting the baby." She told Kevin she miscarried in May 2002 and fell into despair. But soon, she began to tell people her ligation had been reversed. The next year, she told her half brother that yet another child had been born brain-dead and that she had had to carry it full term.

Though Lisa was mentally ill her entire adult life, she did not always suffer the effects of her illness in the same way. Sometimes, she seemed to grasp, at least at some level, that she was not carrying a child. But just as quickly, she seemed convinced that she was. Other times, it was hard to tell what she thought. Maybe she was pregnant but someone else was carrying her child. Maybe she was pregnant but the child had already been born. Her illness did not reveal itself in ways that made sense—to her or to the outside world.

In the spring of 2004, she said she was pregnant yet again. Fortunately, this pregnancy looked more promising. She told a coworker she was "carrying this one ok... my body's not rejecting it." Sometimes she said she was having a boy. Other times it was a girl. Sometimes she was expecting twins; other times she said she had lost one of the twins. She fretted about money for the baby. Carl had given her two dogs in lieu of child support and though she already had three jobs, she hatched a wild plan to become a dog breeder, believing this would solve the family's financial woes. She was even more absent from her children than usual, alternating between obsessing over the dogs and retreating to her room for days at a time. The imaginary pregnancy progressed. The vomiting of the first trimester had passed. Her stomach and breasts seemed to get bigger. She wore loose clothing. She talked about purchasing a home birthing kit and complained about lower back pain. She bought baby items from Toys "R" Us and filed for maternity leave. She received a form from the Kansas Department of Health to register her pregnancy.

As the pregnancy continued, Lisa began to feel overwhelmed. She was trying unsuccessfully to juggle three part-time jobs, four children, two dogs, and a husband who was convinced he was about to become a father. She drove to dog shows throughout the summer. As summer turned to fall and the weather grew cold, she made the bizarre decision to bring the dogs into the house, even though they were not house-trained. The house reeked of dog feces and urine. The children were dirty and neglected. Lisa was exhausted and irritable. She began to feel trapped.

In November, as her due date approached, Carl told Lisa he was going to fight her for custody of the children. He had never been good at paying child support, but now he said he had a big settlement coming from a work injury, and as soon as the check cleared, he was going to take the kids away. He repeated the threat as Lisa's pregnancy progressed, and he insisted the older children were in his corner. Lisa became increasingly desperate. By December, she was falling apart. She took a day off from work but sat at home, paralyzed with distress and unable to function. She was approaching the due date for a child that would never arrive. The dog breeding, like all her other plans, had come to naught. The house was in shambles. The children she loved more than anything had been all but abandoned.

Finally, on December 15, Carl said he would disclose Lisa's history of phony pregnancies to the court and use it to get custody of the children. In one stroke, Carl would not only take her children; he would also reveal to the world that Lisa's identity was built on a lie. And that's how others would likely have seen it—as a lie. Rather than recognizing Lisa's false pregnancies as the sincere but delusional belief of a mentally ill woman, she would be cast out as a charlatan. Lisa would be without children or community, and mocked as a fraud.

But somewhere in Lisa's mind, she could see a solution. When she gave birth, all her problems would be solved. Carl and Judy would see that she *had* been pregnant. It wasn't a lie, it was a miracle. A newborn would protect her other children and give her a precious infant to love and raise as her own. This time would be different. Everyone would see. Everything would be better once the baby came. Later in the day on the fifteenth, Lisa drove to a hospital to deliver her baby, and sat in the parking lot for three hours, crying uncontrollably. Yet she could not bring herself to go inside and could not articulate what she would have said if she had.

The next morning, Lisa contacted Bobbi Jo Stinnett, a dog breeder she had met earlier in 2004. Lisa knew that Stinnett was eight months pregnant because Stinnett had mentioned her pregnancy on her website. Using a false name, Lisa tricked Stinnett into giving Lisa her address by feigning interest in her dogs. The two arranged to meet at Stinnett's home in Skidmore, Missouri. When Lisa arrived midday on December 16, she had a white cord and a sharp kitchen knife concealed in her jacket. After spending a couple of hours visiting with Stinnett and her dogs, Lisa strangled her to death with the cord, cut the fetus from her body with the knife, and claimed the child as her own. She called her Abigail, the name her cousin Wendy said she would use for her next daughter. The police had little difficulty tracking Lisa down and arrested her the next day. She promptly confessed. Investigators later established that prior to the murder, Lisa had been using the Internet to research birth by C-section. Miraculously, the child survived and was returned to Ms. Stinnett's family, who named her Victoria Jo.

5.
"The disquieting complexity of ourselves"

If we ask what Lisa Montgomery did that landed her in prison, the answer is that she brutally murdered an innocent woman, stole her child, and caused indescribable pain. Bobbi Jo Stinnett's family described Ms. Stinnett as "a sweet and loving wife, daughter and sister, and would have been a wonderful mother." These are facts that should never be forgotten or diminished. But if we ask what happened that led Lisa to commit this horrible crime, the answer is far more complicated. To ask what happened is to wonder, with curiosity and compassion, what brought a human being to a particular place. The question widens the lens, like a camera that slowly retreats from a scene to reveal the details that help us make sense of the senseless, bringing an entire life into focus and opening our eyes to the frailty of humanity and the furthest reaches of causation.

To ask what happened insists on the vital difference between an explanation and an excuse. Under ordinary circumstances, we don't have much trouble understanding this difference: One accounts while the other absolves. But when confronted with a great wrong, the unforgiving society deliberately obscures this distinction. It conflates the two and denounces any attempt to understand as a subversive plot to escape blame. At Lisa's trial, the prosecutors mocked her history as "some kind of mental defense to excuse her conduct." One prosecutor could bring himself to admit that it was "unfortunate" Lisa's stepfather had raped her hundreds of times but insisted that her history cannot "be used as an excuse for a savage crime."[11]

What happened to Lisa Montgomery did not cause her to attack Bobbi Jo Stinnett, at least not in the way that gravity causes a coin to fall to the ground when you drop it from your hand. Yet everyone except the most willfully cold would agree that but for this history, Lisa would not have murdered Stinnett. What was done to her, and what she did to survive it, changed her. It narrowed her mental and moral vision and forced her in directions and to choices that seemed sensible only in her imagined reality. Once she reached that fateful day, she chose to act. But fate did not lead her to that day randomly.

Society's insistence that a crime is incomprehensible often conceals its own role in the result. Jack Kleiner raped Lisa because she was an unprotected girl. Because the adults in her life could not or would not protect her, Lisa developed survival strategies that allowed her to endure chaos and pain no one should be forced to endure. Yet these same strategies—dissociation and appeasement—made it appear that Lisa was a bad girl who enjoyed illicit sex and who destroyed her mother's marriage. When she buckled under the weight of her mental illness, people saw her both as a bad mother who could not care for her children, and as a bad woman who destroyed the uniquely feminine and socially sacred bond between a mother and her child. Lisa was judged for what she did but also for her failure to meet society's expectations of how a good girl, mother, and woman should behave.

To judge Lisa Montgomery in a spirit of forgiveness does not yield a number, as though the forgiving society were 36 percent less severe than its opposite. It produces an orientation, a way of understanding society and its members, which includes those who betray it as much as those betrayed by it. This orientation takes its shape from the countless interactions between transgressors and the society that would hold them to account. An observer who knew nothing of a forgiving society would watch these interactions and say that this is a people that does not judge until it first struggles to understand. It does not dwell excessively on either the failings of the individual or the society of which she is a part. Instead, it accepts the challenge of understanding and giving effect to the tangled history that binds each to the other, for in meeting this challenge, the forgiving society reveals and honors the shared humanity of all who live within it.

Lisa Montgomery was not innocent. She was something much more. She was a human being: complex, damaged, and broken. She was a perpetrator, and she was a victim. The struggle to comprehend and give effect to all this—to grasp fully the tangled complexity of her life, of her humanity—is not a subterranean ploy to excuse her. It is something far more ambitious and vital. It is an effort to understand and accept the truth. As James Baldwin wrote more than half a century ago, truth implies "a devotion to the human being." A human being "is not, after all, merely a member of a Society or a Group or a deplorable conundrum to be explained by Science. [S]he is…something more than that, something resolutely indefinable, unpredictable."[12]

The unforgiving society would have us turn our back on the truth. It behaves as though compassion and empathy were zero-sum and bemoans the thought that we might acknowledge the complexity of causation and the frailty of humanity, fearing that it will soften our heart and incline us to judge Lisa in a spirit of forgiveness rather than in an insensate fury. In the place of this compassionate but complex truth, many people substitute the dime-store image of Lisa as a monster, which allows them to shut their mind to their greatest fear: In all the ways that matter, Lisa Montgomery is no different from you or me. But their fear is their weakness, and Baldwin had it right: Lisa's complexity "is nothing more than the disquieting complexity of ourselves." As he wrote, "In overlooking, denying, evading [her] complexity, we are diminished and we perish; only within this web of ambiguity, paradox, this hunger, danger, darkness can we find at once ourselves and the power that will free us from ourselves."[13]

An unforgiving society asks, "What did you do?" It narrows our focus and closes our mind. A forgiving society asks, "What happened? What brought you to this place?" It broadens our inquiry and opens our heart, placing an act into the trajectory of a life filled with pain and promise. To ask what happened is to insist, against all who insist otherwise, that the struggle to comprehend the seemingly incomprehensible is indispensable, for once we understand, we grasp our own humanity.

In 2007, Lisa Montgomery was convicted of capital murder and sentenced to die. She was executed by the United States government January 13, 2021.

CHAPTER 5

"WHAT IF IT'S JUST HUMAN BEINGS?"

> On Jan. 12, 1981, at about 12:10 A.M., Robert Walsh, a NYC Police Officer off-duty was at the B.V.D. Bar & Grill located at 54–02 Flushing Avenue, Maspeth, N.Y. Shortly after 12:10 A.M., three individuals wearing stocking masks over their heads and pointing guns entered the B.V.D. lounge and announced a stickup. When the defendants announced the stickup, the victim took out his badge and identified himself as a NYC Police Officer, whereupon the defendant Richard Rivera shot him once in the shoulder. At this point, the victim fell to the floor, the defendant Richard Rivera then fired another shot hitting the victim in the head.
>
> —PRESENTENCE REPORT, *People of the State of New York v. Richard Rivera* (1982)

1.

"Operating in that level, you're just a creature."

Speaking with Richard Rivera is like talking with an air traffic controller in the tower whose colleagues have all quit. He listens intently and responds thoughtfully, even while he's checking his phone, answering a text, responding to an email, and rescheduling a meeting. Then he gets up, wraps you in a bear hug that cracks your spine in three places, and heads out the door to pick somebody up or drop something off. He takes on new projects as though his life depended on it. As though he were making up for lost time. At sixty, he is still tall, angular, and muscled, with smooth skin that makes him look younger than he is. He has the quick speech and thick accent of Puerto Rican Brooklyn. He punctuates his sentences with the rhetorical question, "you know what I mean?" but if you could write the way he talks, it would be "nwudimean?" with all the letters scrunched together. We were in a coffee shop, talking about prison.

"I started begging in the streets for money," he said. "That's how it started. I was begging for money in the streets when I was, like, eight, seven years old, some shit like that. And I was doing that to help feed my family." He closed his eyes and recalled a scene more than five decades earlier. "Because my sister—one time, we were walking down a hallway and somebody opened up a door and it's the smell of chicken noodle soup that just wafted out at that point. And my little sister, Jenny, just stood there with her face, just this hungry look." He winced at the memory. "And that shit, that image is burned in my mind."

It's not a straight line, of course—the line that connects the seven-year-old child begging in the streets to the sixteen-year-old boy in jail for murder—but the arc is familiar. "One thing leads to another, right? So, you start hustling in the street, then you steal something from the store. Then you steal a car radio. Then you get somebody to buy for you, and then you start getting high with your friends 'cause you got a little crew. And then this, this ratcheting process happens. So, I'm in a crew, and we're just hanging out and stealing stuff. And then I go and punch somebody in the face, right? And suddenly I'm elevated in that culture."

Richard was born in Massachusetts, but he moved with his family to Puerto Rico when he was three. That's where things started to unravel. His parents separated, and he moved with his mother, two brothers, and a younger sister to the Bronx, where they lived briefly with his mother's sister. "It was a dump. It was drug infested, heroin-using place, and the next thing I remember is people shooting dope. People putting ice on their nuts when they were OD'ing, some shit like that." It was 1968. Richard was four. Heroin was flooding into the streets of New York in the late 1960s and early 1970s, first from Marseilles—the French Connection—and later from Sicily, then from Vietnam and Southeast Asia.[1] His aunt was addicted and quickly decided she didn't want another family interfering with her habit. She kicked them out, and they were living under the stairs in a tenement. His mother eventually got an apartment, and "that's when she met Ariel, Ariel Hernandez," who became Richard's stepfather. "He was using heroin to avoid the draft. [His] whole family was doing that shit."

As often as I've talked with Richard about his childhood, when he reaches this point he skips ahead, condensing a decade into a few sentences. "At that time, I'm like five, six. And that's how it started. The rest is me living in the street, dropping out of school, moving from neighborhood to neighborhood. My mom has several psychological episodes, institutionalized—" He says this last part matter-of-factly, the way someone else might mention a summer trip to grandma's house. I pressed him for details, but Richard is vague. "The stress of being beat up and the kids and her husband taking the money. [Hernandez] used to take our welfare checks. Beat her up and take the welfare check. Then I'd go out and hustle some Kentucky Fried Chicken, some shit like that."

Gradually, I learned why a child who was too small to ride the roller coaster at Coney Island was surviving alone on the streets of New York. "He used to beat the shit out of us. All the time." He was talking about Hernandez, and I could tell it was hard for him. "Beat up my mother all the time." Even as a small child, Richard tried pitifully to defend his mother. "Then he'd beat the shit out of me." Fists. Extension cords. Metal hangers. "The coat hangers were the worst," Richard said. "I used the cockroach defense. Lie on my back and flail my arms and legs, some shit like that." I once made the mistake of suggesting that Richard was glossing over his own history, but I didn't appreciate how hard it was for him to recount it. Besides, he said, what was unimaginable for me "was completely normalized" for him. This was just the stuff of his childhood, his every day. Hernandez once punched Richard in the face for mispronouncing the Spanish word for avocado. I asked him how old he was at the time. "Around five, six."

As bad as the beatings were, it was even worse when Hernandez beat Richard's mother behind locked doors. He could hear her screams, hear the sound of Hernandez's fists finding their target, hear her crashing into the furniture and falling to the floor, but could not come to her defense. Many years later, the sound of correctional officers beating someone in another cell, while Richard was locked in his own cell and powerless to intervene, triggered flashes of memory. His skin would flush hot and his heart would pound as he screamed at an unseen CO to stop, as he had screamed at Hernandez so many years before.

"So, that's why I was on the streets," he said. "To get away from the house. Stay out till 2 a.m. Then he'd beat the shit out of me the next morning for staying out late." He was on the streets to escape Hernandez, but also to hustle food. Richard's mother was in and out of mental hospitals throughout his childhood, but the longest stint was when he was about seven. Richard remembers she was hospitalized for months; his mother told a probation officer it was a year. When she was gone, there was no one to fight Hernandez for the welfare check. "There was no food in the house." So, he took to the streets.

And that's where he became a survivor. "I'm stealing, I'm hiding. I'm hanging out by myself all the time, walking through places by myself, hitching buses, hustling over here. Coming home, going back out. I'm randomly operating, just getting money and strategizing and figuring problems out. But it's not an identity. That's just the way human beings move to survive, right? . . . Operating in that level, you're just a creature. There's no self-reflection. There's just a movement to survive."

He started drinking at fourteen—milk and amaretto, because it was sweet—the same year he started smoking weed and the same year he tried to kill his stepfather. Hernandez had beat up his mother for the umpteenth time. "My mom kicked him out . . . and I got a shotgun. Sawed-off shotgun. I'm sitting on the stairs in the tenement building. He comes through the door . . . and I shoot." He missed. He started doing cocaine when he was fifteen, "something I would do three or four times a week." It took a lot of money to support that kind of habit, a lot more than he could get hustling on the street or stealing car radios. He and a group of friends started robbing taverns, which is what they were doing on January 12, 1981, when he shot and killed off-duty police officer Robert Walsh at the B.V.D. Bar in Queens. He was sixteen.

When I went back to the recordings of my conversations with Richard, I was struck by how often he said that when he got to prison, he "didn't have an identity." "I not only could not read or write, I didn't know who I was as an individual. We sort of argue, 'Hey, everybody's got a personality, everybody's got an individuality,' and you think we're born with these things, but these things are constructed over time." But Richard had nothing to construct an identity *from*. It's not just the memories that were never created—his mother never read him a book and his stepfather never took him to the zoo—it's the sense of safety and belonging that he never had. He never heard that he was loved, couldn't have said if it were true, and wouldn't have known what it meant. "So, when I went to prison, all I knew was hunger, pain, getting high, not knowing where I stood, disruption in the household, moving over and over again. There's no ability to create a cohesive identity, and in prison, I did this."

2.

"I was just scared to death. I was scared to death all the time."

A maximum-security prison in this country is a bizarre, dystopian place. It makes people who have almost nothing pay for almost everything, which turns basic necessities into precious commodities and creates a culture of violence. It starts with food. A 2018 study found that, on average, states pay less than $4.00 on food per prisoner per day. Not per meal, per day. In some states, it's substantially less. Alabama pays about $2.00 on food per inmate per day. Wisconsin pays $1.02 a day to feed each person in custody.[2] But though prison portions are notoriously tiny, the real problem is not quantity but quality. Study after study confirms what every person in prison already knows: You can't survive on the pasty glump of nutritional nothingness they serve in the mess hall. It's highly processed, cheaply prepared, and nearly inedible. In one study, the people locked up reported they "rarely or never" have access to fresh fruit or vegetables, and three in four say they have been served food that had already gone bad. A survey in New York found that more than nine in ten prisoners avoid eating meals in the mess hall whenever they can.[3]

But what's the alternative? Some people get occasional food packages from home, but it's never enough to feed a person for their entire prison sentence. That means people have to survive on food from the prison commissary. But the commissary is notoriously expensive. For many items, people pay more in prison than they would on the outside. In 2022, a package of hot dogs in Attica Correctional Facility in New York cost $5.00. A head of lettuce was $3.75. That may or may not sound like a lot of money, but you have to remember that no prisoner in the United States earns anything close to the minimum wage. A 2017 study found that inmates who work in the most common prison jobs across the country—laundry, food service, maintenance, and groundskeeping—make on average between fourteen and sixty-three cents an hour. And that's before mandatory deductions for court-ordered fees, fines, or victim restitution, which can easily take more than half a prisoner's pay.

Though New York is one of the most expensive states in the country, it has one of the lowest prison-wage scales. Most people in New York prisons make between ten and thirty-three cents an hour—again, before mandatory deductions—which means if you're at the top of the scale, you have to work twelve hours to buy a head of lettuce. At the bottom of the scale, you have to work all week. But at least in New York you get paid a few pennies for your labor, which is more than they can say in Alabama, Arkansas, Georgia, Florida, South Carolina, and Texas, which do not pay at all for the most common prison jobs.[4]

A few studies have tried to figure out how much money people need in order to survive in prison. Just for commissary items, the answer is about $100 a month, more in some states, less in others, which means if you're at the top of the prison-wage scale in New York, you have to work ten hours a day, every day, to scrape by. At the bottom, you have to log one thousand hours a month, which works out to about thirty-three hours a day. And that's just to pay for the stuff you can buy from the commissary, like food, hygiene items, or a fan. (In Mississippi, where most prisons do not have air-conditioning, an eight-inch electric fan costs $30. In Georgia, where most prison labor is unpaid, a ten-inch fan costs $32.)[5] The $100 that a person needs for commissary doesn't count, for instance, the cost of medical care. Forty states charge prisoners a copay for every medical visit. These fees typically range from $2 to $5 per visit, so a single trip to see a nurse could cost a week's wages. Texas has the distinction of charging the highest copay—$13.55 per visit—though it does not pay people for the most common prison jobs.[6]

Though advocacy campaigns have forced prisons to lower the price of a phone call over the last fifteen years, in most states a prisoner still has to work all day to pay for a fifteen-minute call. In New York, one study found that people inside spent even more on phone calls and mail than they did on commissary items.[7] In fact, virtually every item that helps a person in prison communicate with the outside world—from stamps, paper, pencils, and envelopes to email—is expensive. For many prisoners, a connection to the world beyond the walls is just another scarce commodity, despite the mountain of evidence that maintaining close contact with family improves mental health and reduces recidivism.

But when I was talking with Richard about scarcity in prison, he helped me understand that it's about so much more than the stuff you can buy at the company store. Everything is for sale. Drugs are a commodity, as is alcohol. Anything that will dull the pain, sharpen the senses, or feed a habit. But so is quiet and a little extra space to enjoy it; you can buy that too, if you can pay the right price to the right people. Working out on this weight pile instead of that one, with these people and not those. Paying someone to create a birthday card for your kid. Talking to your mother on an unmonitored phone. Illegal gambling is present in every prison. Sex is a commodity that people either buy or take. Hiring a lawyer costs a lot of money. So does safety, which might be the most precious good of all. There's a market for everything. Sometimes the seller is another person inside; sometimes it's a correctional officer; sometimes it's a CO on the payroll of a person inside, but it's all for sale. Bartered goods swirl through every prison, all the time. The entire underground economy is against the rules, but everyone participates in it because no one can survive without it. Scarcity is everywhere and everything, all the time.

As it does everywhere, scarcity in prison breeds violence. Since everything is in short supply, everything you own is valuable to someone. All the money in your commissary account, of course, but also the food in your cell, the clothes on your back, and the skills at your command. Your fists are a resource to someone, and so is your body. People inside are at constant risk of being victimized or extorted. And because you can't call a cop to protect you or your belongings, you need to signal to everyone that you are not to be fucked with, which means you have to establish a reputation for violence. And there's no better way to establish that reputation than by being violent. But it's not like you can establish your reputation once and be done with it. As Richard once explained to me, "This is the rule. This is honest to God: Every year you gotta set a new standard. So, if I hit this guy with a shovel today…, the next day you gotta hit somebody with a rock in a sock or knife him, or cut that dude, you know what I mean? You want people to say, 'whoa, that guy's out of control.' But the thing is, you're not gonna be the only one out of control."

It's not impossible for people to stay out of trouble in a maximum-security prison. Every now and again, a person will serve decades and never get in a fight and never get written up by a CO. But it doesn't happen often, and it requires a rare combination of factors that most people never achieve. Most of all, people inside have to have a reliable source of outside financial support, which allows them to buy what they want from the commissary and avoid some of the most dangerous and unpredictable places in the prison. I have a good friend who I met when he was serving seventeen years in a super-maximum-security prison. He never got a disciplinary ticket. He told me he didn't set foot in the mess hall for the last ten years of his bid, both because the food was so bad and because the mess hall was the site of so much random, unprovoked chaos. For him, it was safer to avoid it altogether. But he could only do this because his family regularly put money on his commissary account, which allowed him to buy food and prepare it in his cell. He also benefited from a friendly CO, who looked the other way when he had more than the authorized amount of food in his cell.

People also have to pay their debts. The underground economy runs on credit, and anyone can fall into debt. The people who get in trouble are the ones who can't or won't pay, which makes them a target. As Richard told me once, "Even the best dudes, in order to survive, he's got to protect his image that he's not entirely bullshit and that he's gonna pay his shit on time." It also helps to be humble. "Being humble is a pass. No one ever wants to beat up a humble person." As with everything in prison, being humble has a very particular meaning. "Like, he's Christian, he doesn't talk to nobody, he's real quiet, he's clean, he's very respectful, he doesn't get engaged in bullshit. He's just trying to go home. And because we all aspire to go home, he becomes the symbol of our aspirations. And we don't want to fuck with him, we don't want to discourage him. And if you do, I'm gonna fuck you up."

But none of this described Richard. He was sixteen when he was arrested and charged as an adult, and seventeen when he got to prison, so his age alone made him a target for physical and sexual assault. He didn't know anyone in prison, which meant he had no reputation and no allies. He had killed a police officer, so there was no chance a CO would give him a break. He had never held down lawful employment, so he had no free world skills he could barter or sell. He had no contact with anyone on the outside, including family, and no money in his prison account. He was a young kid with no skills, no friends, and no money, and he was terrified. Early in his bid, he was sent to Great Meadow Correctional Facility in Comstock, New York, a place so renowned for violence that people inside call it the Gladiator School. "I had no friends and no reputation," he said. "I was just scared to death. I was scared to death all the time. I got into so many fights that I lost count after the first month."[8]

And in his fear, he reverted to what he knew. Drugs. Violence. Extortion. For many years, Richard Rivera was among the most violent prisoners in the New York prison system. He did what he thought he needed to do. Yet, whenever I talked with him about the warping effect of scarcity and the ubiquity of violence, whenever we talked about the drugs and the alcohol and the stabbings, about his long stints in the box and his countless fights in the yard, he would add a qualifier. Though brutality and scarcity were everywhere, there was something else too. "You have to remember, this was only ten years after Attica."

3.

"I go up there looking for Socrates in the S section."

In his tightly woven account of the crack epidemic, Donovan X. Ramsey reminds us that "all events are the result of countless others, big and small, coming together at a particular moment. They pile up like logs on a pyre. Then there's some kindling, a spark...and suddenly, a fire." Though he was talking about the crack epidemic, he could've just as easily been describing the lead-up to the Attica uprising. Conditions in Attica had been horrific for as long as the men inside could remember. Prisoners got one shower a week and one roll of toilet paper a month. COs were brutal, and "the goon squad" bludgeoned inmates with impunity. Complaints fell on deaf ears.[9]

At the same time, the radicalism of the 1960s and early 1970s had begun to penetrate New York prisons. In the summer of 1971, five men in Attica created the Attica Liberation Front (ALF) to try to improve conditions inside the walls. As one of the founders would later recall, "We started teaching political ideology to ourselves. We read Marx, Lenin, Trotsky, Malcolm X, Du Bois, Frederick Douglass and a lot of others."[10] The ALF held open classes and study groups throughout the prison, which provided people with a forum to discuss the conditions they endured and gave them a political perspective on why those conditions never got better.

In July 1971, the ALF wrote a letter to the New York Commissioner of Corrections and the warden at Attica, calling for better conditions. The warden responded by increasing the frequency of cell searches and censoring all discussion of prison conditions, which continued to deteriorate throughout the summer. On September 8, COs took two men to solitary confinement, and a rumor went around that they had been beaten to death. The next day, a small group of prisoners was being held in a tunnel and believed the goon squad was going to descend on them. They overpowered four COs and locked them in cells. The uprising had begun.

The ALF drafted a list of demands, which opened with this proclamation: "We are *men*! We are not beasts and we do not intend to be beaten or driven as such."[11] Negotiations with the administration continued for several days, but on September 13, while negotiations were still underway, New York governor Nelson Rockefeller ordered hundreds of heavily armed troops to retake the facility. Officers on the rooftop gunned down prisoners in the yard, who had no firearms. They killed twenty-eight prisoners and eleven hostages. Scores of prisoners were shot but survived; hundreds more were brutalized by officers after the uprising had been crushed. Then came the lies and the cover-up. New York officials falsely claimed the hostages had been killed by inmates, denied the torture and beatings their own men had inflicted, and hid evidence for decades.

After the uprising, the administration transferred hundreds of prisoners from Attica to Green Haven Correctional Facility, an hour north of New York City. After what they had just survived, these men were more determined than ever to carry on and expand the revolutionary spirit that had existed in Attica. A group of them created the Think Tank, a legendary prison organization that focused on improving conditions and educating fellow inmates. Led by Eddie Ellis, a cofounder of the New York chapter of the Black Panther Party who would go on to become a national leader in prison reform, the Think Tank created study groups similar to those that had existed in Attica.[12] The Think Tank was a vibrant political and intellectual hub by the time Richard got to Green Haven in 1984. "There was a real philosophy of 'each one teach one,'" he told me. This was no empty slogan; it was a moral and political obligation, and members of the Think Tank took Richard under their wing. "The dudes you read about in *Blood in the Water*,* I shook hands with them, I hugged them, I ate with them. Eddie Ellis was my mentor."

Members of the Think Tank may have been Richard's friends and mentors, but they were not above a little tough love. "When I got to prison, all I wanted to do was get high and play football." There was an inmate football league at Green Haven, but none of the coaches would draft him. Richard soon discovered they were acting on orders from the Think Tank, one of whose members explained to Richard that he couldn't play football until he got his GED. Richard being Richard, he "punched him in the face." But he made the mistake of punching Theodore ("T") Haywood, a former boxer. "He kicked my ass." Richard decided he would get his GED. (Haywood, who was serving a life sentence for murder, would eventually be released and become the lead mentor at the Osborne Association, a New York nonprofit that serves people hurt by the criminal legal system.)

Richard's first challenge was to learn to read. Another Attica survivor had tried to teach Richard to read shortly after he was arrested. He introduced Richard to the radical Black protest literature that had been so important at Attica, reading to him from *Soledad Brother*, the

* *Blood in the Water* is the Pulitzer Prize–winning account of the uprising by the historian Heather Thompson.

collected letters of activist and revolutionary George Jackson written when Jackson was in Soledad Prison in California. It had been Jackson's murder by correctional officers in August 1971 that helped trigger the uprising days later in Attica. "He would read [the letters] to me, then I would follow the words. Say, 'what's this word? What's that mean?' Every letter that *Soledad Brother* contains? He made me recopy every letter." But Richard wasn't ready to be a reader, and he told me the instructions "didn't take." It wasn't until he got to Green Haven that reading became a lifelong passion. He can still remember the first book he ever read. "*Rage of Angels*, a novel by Sidney Sheldon. I was so proud of myself."

But he didn't spend long on fictional tales of seduction and intrigue. "Then I went back to Angela Davis, *If They Come in the Morning*," he said, referring to a collection of essays edited by Davis with contributions by, among others, Huey Newton and Bobby Seale, the cofounders of the Black Panther Party. "Then I finally got through *Soledad Brother*." But there were many others: *Soul on Ice*, by Eldridge Cleaver. *Native Son*, by Richard Wright. The essays of James Baldwin. *The Autobiography of Malcolm X*.

Richard got his GED in Green Haven and was celebrating with his friends and a plateful of cocaine in the mess hall when talk turned to Durkheim and Socrates. His friends got into a debate "and it was like really complicated and I don't understand what the fuck was going on." He asked a friend, "Who the fuck is Socrates? 'He's that philosopher, man.' And he's high with me, we're talking shit. I said, 'Look, I gotta get a book in the library, man.' So, I go up there looking for Socrates in the S section. Come back. Say, 'what the fuck you mean? There's no book by Socrates.' Dude say, 'No, you gotta read Plato.'" So, he did. All of it. "I think I picked up *The Apology* first. Read that, and then I end up reading all his books and eleven letters of Plato. Everything Plato ever wrote."

Another innovation of the Think Tank was to form a collaboration with Marist College near Poughkeepsie, which became the first school to offer college courses in New York prisons. Richard, who could not read a word when he got to prison in 1982, became a college student in 1987. His first class was Introduction to Anthropology. "Midterms come, and I get an F. Guy says to the class, 'I want you to write in a way that you could explain these ideas to an eight-year-old.' And that's what I did. On my final, I got an A." He was hooked. "I went and hit the books again. I started reading the books seriously." Anthropology gave way to philosophy. "I took a class with an existentialist philosopher and he called me a Platonist at one point. I thought he said plagiarist and I passed out. Made a fool out of me." He chuckles at the memory. Richard would eventually get a bachelor's degree in philosophy and a master's degree in divinity, although that was still decades in the future.

By the late-1980s, Richard said he was "a well-known entity" in Green Haven. On one hand, he was a drug dealer and extortionist who had overcome the scarcity of prison by mastering the culture of violence. "I'm getting alcohol from the police. I'm in the system now. I'd tell the COs, 'Yo, bring me two bottles of blackberry brandy.' They'd bring it in. Lot of weed. One time I had so much weed, I had a radio about this big"—he held his hands about ten inches apart—"I had to gut it to put all my weed inside." On the other hand, he was a college student and a voracious reader with an interest in Plato and radical Black political theory, under the tutelage of Attica survivors, most of whom, like Richard, were serving life sentences for murder. At the time, he didn't give much thought to these head-spinning contradictions. It was just life on the inside.

But change was coming. "In Green Haven, people start disappearing."

4.

"We used to call it The Monster."

Those who lived through it will never forget the fear that gripped society during the early years of the AIDS epidemic, when a sore throat made your stomach turn and a diagnosis was a death sentence. But as terrifying as the epidemic was on the outside, it was infinitely worse in prison. Everyone at Green Haven had a theory, a strategy that would keep them safe. Some thought a mouthful of raw garlic would kill the virus. Others said it was a government conspiracy, which meant you couldn't eat food from the mess hall or accept medication from the nurses. Then there was Popeye. "Popeye had these big floppy ears," Richard said. "Old-timer. Heroin user. Intravenous drug user. He used to come out every night with rolled up magazines to kill mosquitoes. This was his thing. He's killing insects because insects are transmitting this. Mosquitoes have blood on them, every time [he] squashed one. That means they're passing them from you to me, you know what I mean?" One summer day, after a heavy rain, Richard found Popeye in the prison bathroom, curled in the filth. "He's in the corner, crying, mumbling to himself with the newspaper, because there's too many mosquitoes out there. He can't get 'em all."

AIDS destroyed the solidarity of the Attica era. The openly gay and transsexual were attacked first. Early in his bid, Richard saw a young man race across the yard carrying a cup of liquid. "He goes to Jessica, this transsexual person, and throws it on her." Then he lit a match, held it to her face, and shouted, "'You're gonna leave this fucking yard, fucking faggot!' And Jessica is *terrified*." That night, she checked herself into protective custody. Her tormentor later tested seropositive for HIV and took his own life. People hid anything that looked or sounded like a symptom. Every sneeze was just an allergy; every cough just throat-clearing. But it was no use: "When an individual would cough or show any symptoms, [they would] get attacked. Get their cells burned out, get cut and told to leave the yard."

AIDS tore through New York prisons. In the mid- to late-1980s, nearly one in five people incarcerated in New York prisons was HIV+, the highest infection rate of any prison system in the country.[13] "We used to call it The Monster," Richard told me. Prisoners who tested positive were removed from the population, and before long, Richard's friends began to disappear. "We didn't know where they were. They were just gone and nobody would tell us anything." Richard especially wanted to track down his friend, David, who had been his mentor at Comstock, the Gladiator School. David had saved Richard when he was about to be cut by an older and much bigger inmate. He then took Richard under his wing and gave him invaluable lessons in the ways of prison life. "He taught me how to do time," Richard said.

After a lot of unanswered questions, a couple of friendly COs—"Puerto Rican dude named Lopez and an African American named Cooper"—finally agreed to show Richard where his friends had gone. They led Richard up to the fourth floor, down an unfamiliar corridor, and past New York's electric chair, which had been transferred to Green Haven from Sing Sing in 1971. They ushered Richard into a large, empty dormitory and led him toward the darkness in the back of the room. A sheet of Plexiglas sliced the room in two, marking the forbidden territory beyond. Lopez opened a gate and allowed Richard to pass inside.

What he saw stopped him cold. There were eight cots, four down one wall, four down the other. Each contained what remained of a man, that part of body and mind that had not yet been devoured by AIDS. Some were staring blankly into space. Others were drifting in and out of AIDS-related dementia. Staff and correctional officers were afraid to come to this makeshift ward, and the stench was nearly unbearable, the stink of human beings left to die alone in their shit and piss and sweat, too weak to clean themselves. And there was his friend David, slack-jawed and emaciated, lying in the dark with sunken, vacant eyes. Puss was leaking from one eye. One leg was swollen nearly to bursting.

Many people would have turned around and not come back. Richard admits that he recoiled. "I was floored." But he did not retreat. He began making regular trips to the ward. Soon, he was visiting every day. The prison let him stay there all morning, and that's what he did. He collected food from people on the tier and brought it to the fourth floor. The prison was all too happy to let Richard play this role. They gave him gloves. He cleaned the puss from people's eyes. Rubbed lotion on their cracked and swollen limbs. Played cards with people who had the strength. Listened to those who could carry on a conversation. Talked to those who could not talk. Held their hands as they drifted in and out of consciousness, and as they died. "Do you know how many guys I've watched die?" he asked me once.

In the AIDS ward, Richard had an epiphany: When so little of a human being is left, nothing but humanity matters. Prison is an intensely stratified space, and people are defined by who they associate with. "Snitches. Black. White. Gang members. Outlaws. Rat hunters. Drug dealers. There's so many categories in prison [and] you are defined by what you choose.... You're defined by the categories you choose to embrace." But in the AIDS ward, these categories lost their meaning. "In that space, that infirmary space, all that shit became nonsensical.... [W]hat I was doing transcended the categories. Helping people who were HIV+, helping our friends out. If I'm helping this guy, why can't I help this [other] guy, you know what I mean? Why can't I do it?"

Richard spent five years working with AIDS patients at Green Haven, going to the infirmary nearly every day. "I'm no longer hanging out and eating doughnuts with the guys that are of the same persuasion." Instead, he was participating in something "that engages the human being and not the category, and that's why it was pivotal in my life." He became a leading advocate for AIDS education in prison, and advised senior prison officials and politicians on how to address the crisis. He was one of the founders of PACE, Prisoners for AIDS Counseling and Education. PACE educators, all of whom are incarcerated, support people who are HIV+ and provide HIV/AIDS education to other people inside. The organization still exists. It operates at facilities throughout New York and has been adopted by prison systems across the country.

Because Richard's work was so positive and so transformative, because it so thoroughly "disrupted [his] perception of things," we want to believe the change it produced was instantaneous, like a light switching on, or that if it was more gradual, it was at least inevitable, like the coming of dawn. But that's not how change happens. Metaphors like this overlook how incredibly difficult it is for someone to abandon the patterns that have sustained them for so many years. Yes, the patterns might be unhealthy and destructive—yes, they might have led us astray time and time again—but they're all we've ever known, and the only thing more terrifying than the thought of living with them is the thought of living without them.

And if change is hard on the outside, it's even harder in a maximum-security prison. After he started ministering to the men dying of AIDS, Richard turned to religion and spirituality to help him comprehend the suffering and death that surrounded him. He read voraciously. The Torah. The Bible. The Koran. He read about Buddhism and the religions of ancient Greece. Anything that would help him understand the pointlessness of it all. He began to meditate. For about eighteen months, he stopped going to the yard and stepped away from the drugs, the extortion, and the violence. He became increasingly ascetic, gave away much of his property, and slept on the floor of his cell. He spent his days going from the infirmary to his cell, tending to the sick and meditating on death.

One day, he went back to the yard. There was a new kid there. He didn't know Richard or his reputation. "This fucking kid, he called me a bitch," Richard said. "'What is your bitch ass doing here?' He actually accused me of hiding from someone. I couldn't have that. So, I went and grabbed a knife, stabbed him up."

When law and order politicians try to make the case for prison or the death penalty, they point to people like Richard. After shooting a police officer in the head, he threatened and extorted hundreds of people, sent untold numbers to the infirmary with serious injuries, and spent a staggering twelve and a half years in the box. And when advocates try to make the case for reform, they point to people like Richard. He developed extraordinary empathy and compassion, along with a universal commitment to human dignity and respect. "I would go to the hospital every day and take care of patients. I'm collecting food from dudes. I say, 'Yo, I'm goin' upstairs to the hospital. Put some food in the bag.' Take it up to the guys in the block. Put lotion on people, take care of them, talk to them for hours. Watch guys die. Watch guys go through AIDS-related dementia. At the same time, I'm in the yard, fighting dudes, going through shit. Participating in the drug culture, everything. Extorting guys. Everything. This is all happening in tandem with each other."

These two worlds cannot live in balance forever. The act of caring for the most vulnerable people in the facility, with no hope or expectation that he would benefit from it, awakened something in Richard, and he liked it. "I go to the hospital, I'm holding guys' hands, I'm talking to them. And I feel good." In the relative quiet of his cell and in the bare life of the infirmary, Richard caught a glimpse of the person he wanted to be. "Then I go to the yard and I do these things." He began to despise the person he was in the yard and slowly came to see himself as the yard's victim rather than its master. "I don't want to do this. Why are you forcing me to do this? These situations, the circumstances, the environment, the attitude, it gets you angry and makes you want to just go rampage, because now you're forcing me to do something, I'm gonna show you what I can do." As he told me on a different occasion, "What's playing out in the prison population is the mask, right? It's the person I need to become to survive in here. What's happening in the cell is the person I hope to become."

But even when he wanted to, Richard found it hard to escape the reality of the yard. In one of our conversations, he told me about a friend inside. "Smarter than I am. But the abuses, the dehumanization, the denigration and the embarrassment after embarrassment after embarrassment. You know what that could do to an individual's psyche? He gets slapped over here in front of those people. When he goes to this prison he gets raped.... That's just the way it's gonna be. And the starving night after night. The hunger in [his] eyes going to sleep night after night." For Richard, the unrelenting pain inflicted on a friend who was doing his time the right way justified Richard taking food from another person who was breaking the unwritten rules: "And then I see this motherfucker here. Punk-ass motherfucker running around here, eating all this shit, has all this money, and he's a snitch. And it justifies [me saying], 'motherfucker, you're going to give me your shit or we're leaving here today.'" Translation: You're either giving me your food so I can feed the guys in the infirmary, or we're going to the yard right now, which will end with you cut and both of us shipped to Upstate Correctional Facility, where we'll be locked down twenty-four hours a day. Take your pick because it makes no difference to me.

In prison, change comes slowly.

5.

"I'm gonna try to live my life in a way that respects and honors that memory."

"I didn't start thinking about my crime until about 25 years," Richard said.

When he said this, I couldn't believe it. I didn't want to believe it. But a maximum-security prison is not a world that encourages reflection. "Most individuals don't get the chance to do that," he said. "They're living on the razor's edge. You have to live in this state of awareness. You expect the screaming. You expect the shit-throwing. You live constantly on the razor's edge. When you go to the shower. Everywhere. Constantly. It's a constant state of anxiety. We live in a place defined by violence and the leader is the one who expresses that best." A maximum-security prison is a world of humiliation, fear, brutality, and hunger. For many people in prison, quiet reflection is just another unaffordable luxury.

Richard couldn't afford this luxury until he had been in prison more than two decades. By then, he had gotten married and his wife put a small amount of money on his commissary account every month. This meant that for the first time, Richard could escape the scarcity of prison without participating in the violence. At the same time, his reputation for violence had spread through the system. After more than twenty years in prison, he was an old-timer in the system, even though he was not yet forty. He could put on the mask whenever he needed to, and no one doubted that he could still be as violent as he was the day he arrived. Ironically, this hard-earned reputation for violence helped keep him safe. And finally, Richard had established a reputation as "a stand-up guy." Word of his work for AIDS patients had gotten around, which people honored for its selflessness. He had never been in a gang and had never been a sexual predator. Plus, people respected his devotion to learning. Putting it all together, after more than two decades, Richard was finally able to carve out a space in prison where he could truly confront the meaning and enormity of his crime.

And for Richard, that was no small thing. To ask, "What happened? What could I have done differently? Those are just reflections." He meant something much more profound. Accepting "total and complete responsibility" for the death of another human being, as Richard did, means "assum[ing] on yourself" the full weight and emotional force of the murder. He came to feel his guilt viscerally, all the pain he caused and the lives he ruined, and experienced it as a deep, internal sensation that flowed through him. "To immerse yourself, to close your eyes and to say, 'okay, this is my deed. This is it. This is what I did.' It takes immersion." In never-ending waves, he experienced "concentric circles of guilt. When you cry, [when] you think about the kids [who won't have a father] ... you start experiencing it as a *thing* that is really immersive."

Richard swears he never meant to shoot anyone. As he tells it, when Walsh shouted that he was a police officer, he startled Richard, who turned quickly, pulled the trigger twice without thinking, and ran out of the bar.[14] But Richard does not shy away from the fact that by his hand alone, Robert Walsh is dead. When he could finally embrace his identity as someone who took another's life, it threw him into "a crisis of belonging." "Who am I? Am I this thing that killed somebody? Then you have to deal with it." He had to try to make it right. But how could he atone for murder? "I committed a horrible crime. I killed a person, right? ... If you reflect on it, it's one of those things that I cannot pay back. I cannot. When you arrive at this point that you accept responsibility for what you did and you want to pay back. But how do I make this right? If I really experience contrition and I want forgiveness and I want to reconcile and I want to make amends for this, how do I move forward from death?"

He looked to religion, but it provided no answer. "In the Christian tradition, I make right with Jesus [and] Jesus makes right with everybody else for me." But that felt too easy, too far removed from genuine atonement. "In the Jewish tradition, I must go to the individual themselves. There's no God gonna help me out. I must go to you and get forgiveness from you." Richard wanted to seek forgiveness from his victim, but that of course was impossible. "That's the difficult part. But that's the position I was in. That's what I wanted to do. So, I get stuck in this situation, existentially stuck, that I cannot move forward because I cannot make amends for what I did. I killed somebody, right?"

Richard said he was stuck in this place for years, wracked with guilt but unable to atone. Eventually, he came to the decision that guides him to this day. "I want to move forward, and I want to move forward in a way that honors and respects my victim." But he didn't know his victim, and New York law prevents him from contacting the victim's family. So, he imagined his victim as the best human being the world has ever known. "The person I murdered could have been the most horrible person in the world. He could have been an alcoholic, beating his wife, raping his kid, I don't know. But in my mind, because I need to move forward, I put the best qualities of [a] human being in this individual. And I'm gonna try to live my life in a way that respects and honors that memory, even if it's a factitious memory, an image in my mind, and that's how I decided to move forward."

"Those are the meanings I found [in prison]," he said. "I found that I have a greater responsibility than to be selfish."

Richard applied for parole after he had been locked up twenty-five years. The parole board turned him down. He applied again two years later, and they turned him down again. And two years after that, and two years after that. They turned him down six times in a row before finally granting him parole on his seventh trip to the board. He was released in 2019, after more than thirty-eight years in custody. He paroled to a small town near Ithaca, New York, where he and I met. Shortly after his release from prison, he made his way to Ithaca's long-time homeless encampment, known locally as the Jungle. During the pandemic, he was there every day, delivering food, clothes, bedding—anything people needed. He began to write and speak about what he saw, which brought him to the attention of the Center for Community Alternatives in New York, which works with people across the state who have been affected by mass incarceration. They hired him in 2024. He develops and administers programs to improve the lives of people reentering society from prison.

I asked Richard to review a draft of this chapter for accuracy. He balked at a line I had written, "What if the sinners are the saints?" He asked me, "What if there are no sinners or saints? What if it's just human beings?"

CHAPTER 6

"HE'S NOT READY"

> The Juarito street gang has terrorized, and continues to terrorize, the streets of Oklahoma City and the metro area by committing numerous crimes including but not limited to homicide, assaults with deadly and dangerous weapons, drive-by shootings, robberies, drug sales, burglaries, theft and witness intimidation.
>
> —AFFIDAVIT OF PROBABLE CAUSE, *State of Oklahoma v. David Medina et al.* (2012)

1.

When David Medina was a child growing up on the southeast side of Oklahoma City, he used to ride his bike into the middle of the street. "And there would be cars driving, and I would purposely, like, want to get seen by them." He would ostentatiously glance at the toy watch on his wrist and then race off, as though he were late for something desperately important. "I wanted people that was seeing me to think I was on my way, speeding to a gang meeting.... I wanted everyone to see that's the mission and focus, and that's what was on." He was seven at the time, maybe eight.

As long as he can remember, David wanted to be in a gang. "Even as a little kid, I just, man, I wanted that. It was just that hunger and thirst and taste of the stuff I would see. I wanted some of that." He and his family later moved to the northwest side of the city, and while other kids in the neighborhood were playing with toys, "in my mind, I was playing like as if I was a gangster." Even in kindergarten he remembers having "bad thoughts. I'm doing bad things. And then I started getting a little bit more older, started, you know, watching, you know, bad movies. Like as far as dealing with gangs and drugs and all of that."

Men who have left gangs often say that older gang members had wooed them with visions of an adrenaline-filled world brimming with all the things a young man could possibly want—money, clothes, women. Others say the gang was a surrogate family, providing the illusion of unconditional love that they couldn't find at home. Still more note that the gang provided some security in a dangerous neighborhood. But none of that applied to David. He didn't need to be lured into the life or protected on the streets, and he wasn't trying to replace his family. He just wanted to be a gangster. He said, "I remember I was in elementary, and ... wanted everyone to think that I was in a gang. And I didn't even know a gang. Like, you know what I mean? I wanted everyone to think that."

"But that doesn't come from nowhere," I interjected. "Where does that come from?" We were sitting in a Panera Bread on the southwest side of Oklahoma City, talking about his life in the gang. No one had ever asked him what drew him to the life, and David had never given it much thought. He paused a few seconds and said, "They say babies' brains are like sponges, and they absorb everything in its path. So picture, as a kid, you're in this environment, if you see a drug deal that just happened, you see [it], or if you've seen some violence that just happened, you observe that, you know what I mean?" As David was coming up, the gangs were everywhere. "I remember clearly, there was plenty of times as a little kid, I would go to the movie theaters and I would see...two different gangs fighting each other." He told me about driving to church with his grandmother. "I would look outside the window, you'll see a crowd of people get chased by another crowd of people....Things like that started becoming a norm for me."

But if we're trying to make sense of David's infatuation with gang life, we can't give all the credit—or blame—to these snapshots from his childhood. He attended church every Sunday but didn't want to become a priest; he went to school every weekday but didn't want to become a teacher; he grew up in a high-crime neighborhood but didn't want to become a cop. There was something about being a gang member that dazzled him and made his heart race in a way that nothing else could touch. When he saw all the dealing and the violence, the mayhem and swagger, it didn't intimidate or frighten him. He was drawn to it, intoxicated by it, and he "wanted a taste of it." Even before he understood what the gangs were, he dressed and strutted the way he thought a gang member would, and carried himself as though he'd been in a gang almost from the moment he emerged from the womb.

I asked him what he found so irresistible about the gangs, and he thought for a moment before answering. "To me at that time, it was, you could say, a person of power." But it wasn't just any power that he craved. He wasn't after some cloaked power that pulled strings from behind the scenes. As he wove through traffic on his bicycle, David wanted to be immensely, unavoidably *visible*. He wanted drivers to see him—he wanted *everyone* to see him—and he wanted them to get out of his way, because in his mind, that's what gang members did—they make everyone else cross to the other side of the street. He wanted his membership in a gang to conjure an image not just in his own mind, but in the mind of everyone around him. I asked him, when drivers saw him as a gang member, what was the picture he wanted them to have in their head? "Now looking back on it, respect stands out as a huge factor, just respect. Where it's like, you know, this respect is needed. If not, there's going to be stuff like consequences for that."

Power and respect. From an early age, David Medina wanted to have power and command respect. I asked him how old he was when he first started carrying a gun. "Ten or eleven," he said. "I was a little kid riding a bike. And some people . . . had disrespected or cussed at me or something. I'm on the bike and I remember I had like a little firearm. And . . . I stopped and started shooting towards them." Power and respect. After our first meeting, David continued to reflect on his answers. It's as if I had asked, "What's the first word you wanted people to think when they saw you as a gang member?" and his answer—*respect*—surprised him. When we met the next day, he said he had been trying to make sense of this childhood obsession. Were there "certain things that I would see, or the environment I was around? Was there, you know, certain things that I missed that, you know, caused certain other things? If I'm demanding respect, so then I would be asking myself now, like, 'Man, why was I demanding respect?'"

But maybe the answer isn't that hard to understand. He told me about the resentment he felt at his family's constant, soul-crushing poverty. To this day, David has never met his biological father. His mother exhausted herself at two jobs and still never seemed to bring home enough money to keep the lights on. There were plenty of days with no food and nights with no heat. At Christmas, he thought it was a blessing if he got any gift at all. The small child who burns with shame at his thrift-store wardrobe, who sneaks off from the grocery store with a cart full of stolen food so he and his family can eat, and whose apt nickname in the gang was Tiny, aspires to the day when he can flash his cash for all to see, when everyone steps out of his way when he walks down the street and children look up at him with slack-jawed wonder. The words that dispel resentment and shame are *power* and *respect*. And in David's neighborhood, the group with the most power—the people who commanded respect and oozed swagger—were not the priests or the teachers or the cops. It was the Juaritos.

2.

Gangs are always recruiting, and David had made it obvious that he was looking to join. Even before he was ten, other gangs had approached him and encouraged him to join, but David turned them away. That fact surprised me, and in my middle-class mindset, I thought his next sentence would be about a little voice that told him he was about to cross a Rubicon and would come to regret it. Nah. All this time, he had been assessing the gangs just as they had been assessing him. He saw the gangs that ran away when they were chased, and like an all-state quarterback who turns up his nose at a Division 3 school, David knew he was destined for something bigger than a gang that ran from a fight. He wanted to be part of a gang that never backed down. He wanted to be a Juarito.

The Juaritos were founded in Oklahoma City in the 1970s by immigrants from Ciudad Juarez, Mexico, and expanded dramatically in the early 1990s when the children born to that first generation began recruiting in the neighborhoods and schools. Police incorrectly thought the gang took its name from a city in Mexico named Juarito, but it's simply one of the many nicknames for someone from Juarez, and the name signaled the gang's historic connection to the city. The Juaritos controlled territory on both the south and northwest sides of Oklahoma City. They weren't the biggest gang in the city, but they were growing rapidly, and the police connected them to a disproportionate share of the city's violence.

David never told anyone that he had shot at people who disrespected him when he was ten or eleven, and it turns out he didn't need to. "I didn't tell nobody about it, but somehow, the gang ended up hearing about it, and they ended up reaching out." The Juaritos were impressed with his moxie, but maybe even more with the fact that he didn't brag about it afterward and wasn't particularly troubled by what he had done. He just went about his business. It would still be years before wisps of beard would appear on his chin, but he was already deadly serious, completely discreet, and stone-cold. He was perfect for the Juaritos, and when they made their pitch, David didn't hesitate. His childhood dream came true in 1996 when he was initiated into the gang. He was twelve.

David was actively involved in the gang from the late-1990s until his arrest in 2012, a period that corresponds with the worst gang violence in Oklahoma City's history. By mid-year 2003, overworked counselors who worked with the Latino community estimated that nearly one-third of the city's homicides could be traced to gang vendettas. Some houses had more bullet holes than windows, and a home in an area controlled by the Juaritos had been shot up every night for a week. Officers with the local gang unit said that warring Latino gangs were "the biggest threat to the city right now," and the police complained that drive-by shootings and gang contract killings were "way up" from the year before.[1] Still, the lure of the gang drew more young people into the life. When a counselor pulled up and honked his horn outside a home festooned with Juaritos graffiti and pocked with bullet holes, six small children appeared in a living room window and quickly began flashing gang signs. A journalist estimated that none of the children were older than five. "It's a war," the counselor observed, "and we're losing."[2]

And it only got worse. In 2003, the police were alarmed when the number of drive-by shootings reached 129. The next year there were nearly 200, including the night in early August when bullets crashed through the window of a home on the northwest side and killed nine-year-old David Pekah, who was sleeping on a love seat in the living room. "It's just a game to them ... shooting things," Pekah's mother said. "They don't care what they do, or what happens to people or families." It was the third time in six months that her house had been shot up. Two of her sons were Juaritos, and she assumed the shooting was in retaliation for another shooting that took place earlier that summer.[3] A few days after Pekah was killed, and in apparent retaliation for his murder, a twenty-three-year-old was shot in the face and killed as he sat in the front seat of his car. Police arrested and charged a member of the Juaritos with the murder, but he was acquitted at trial when the eye-witness testimony fell apart. "That's the problem with these drive-by shootings," his lawyer said after the verdict. "There are a thousand gangbangers on the south side of Oklahoma City. It could be anybody."[4]

Police responded to the escalating violence in late 2004 with a sweep that netted sixty-five gang members. At a press conference announcing the arrests, Oklahoma County Sheriff John Whetsel said, "You can run, but you can't hide. That's really the message to gang members. In Oklahoma County, we're going to do everything we can to take you off the street."[5] Yet, the following year, the number of drive-by shootings climbed to 260, more than double the number in 2003, followed by another 245 in 2006.[6] In 2007, the Oklahoma City Police Department acknowledged the "dramatic increase in gang-related violence" since the beginning of the century, and the Oklahoma state legislature found that gang violence was "decimating the lives of many youths and families."[7] That same year, Oklahoma City was one of only four cities in the country chosen to receive special funding from the Department of Justice to help combat gang violence. Between 2004 and 2008, a larger fraction of Oklahoma City's homicides were gang related than in any major city in the country except Los Angeles and Long Beach.[8]

But statistics like this only begin to capture the chaos that engulfs a single life. From about the age of thirteen or fourteen, David was in nearly constant trouble with the law. "I remember I would get locked up to the juvenile facility, get out, go right back in. Then I would get sent to [long-term juvenile] placement. They would send me to places where I had to do time. I would get out from that, go back. And I just kept escalating." I asked him what he was doing that got him in trouble, and he answered with a laundry list. "It would start from like burglary, vandalism.... Let's say if we're in a stolen vehicle, spray painting on walls, having stuff in my possession that I'm not supposed, whether it's certain types of drugs, firearms."

Before long, he was completely engulfed in the life. On a "normal day"—if such a thing existed—"you're already prepared for war. There's not even no rest. No sleep. You're just, you know what I mean, on combat mode." In 2004, David was shot in the face and back, and he flatlined three times before he stabilized. He had to relearn how to walk and talk, and still has pieces of shrapnel lodged in his skull. Yet this did not remotely shake his allegiance to the gang, and as he lay in the hospital, all he could think about was retaliation. I asked him the goal of all this violence, expecting him to say that it was about claiming and controlling territory. But if that was an objective, it was secondary. The real goal was just "to win. To have dominance over others... defeat others."

And he pursued that goal relentlessly. "The way my mind was at the time, it didn't matter where I was at." He recently stopped at an intersection and his mind flashed back "to whenever I was living that life and it's like, I would be out there, just like it is right now, it'd be bright, no matter how many vehicles are out there, if I'm at an intersection and if I'm next to someone that is from a rival gang, I'm gonna try to shoot. And that's how my mind was at the time. I didn't care about who was gonna see me. I didn't care about the possibilities of what could happen. All I was focused on was like, I need to get this person."

He and a few other Juaritos eventually moved into a home on the northwest side of the city. "Our block was like a world war," David said. "There's constant shootings happening. Our house is getting shot at, or, if we're out there and we notice someone and we're shooting at [them]. Now that I look back, I'm like, poor families, you have stray bullets just going crazy." But this concern for the welfare of bystanders is something he feels only in retrospect. I asked him what he *did* feel in place of concern, and he said, "I didn't think anything of them. I didn't have no thoughts of them. It's like, if you picture someone in a dark tunnel, and there's just darkness in this tunnel, but it's covered, and you cannot see what's on the outside of that concrete. That's pretty much how I was walking and seeing. Your eyes can see it but not see it."

Yet at least some Juaritos *did* see it. They saw the neighbors they were endangering and made sure none of them called the police. As a member of the Oklahoma City Gang Task Force would later write, the Juaritos "intimidate good citizens from cooperating with the police by threats and acts of violence." During the investigation against the gang, "numerous accounts were found of the Juaritos terrorizing and intimidating good citizens in the neighborhood so that they would not call or cooperate with the police."

In the months before he was arrested, David told me it felt like he was attending a funeral "almost every week." But all he could feel was a retaliatory fury. "I have an anger. It's like a pain is coming, but I don't know how to deal with it. . . . It's like I have this coldness. I'm looking at my friend, I'm seeing his mom crying and it immediately turns to anger. And now I have this rage. Now I'm furious. I'm seeing the suffering and I'm like, man, I want them to suffer. I want the same tears to happen, you know what I mean?"

I asked him how he would've described himself during this period. He paused for a second, drew a breath, and said, "At that time, an evil person."

"You would've described yourself as an evil person?"

"And that's what I wanted people to see."

"You wanted people to see you as evil?"

"Yeah."

"You *wanted* people to see you as evil."

"Yeah."

"What does that mean?"

"Doing anything and everything that is bad, that is dark."*

For years, David Medina was a high-ranking member of one of the largest and most violent street gangs in Oklahoma City. He and his brothers in the gang imported and distributed mountains of illegal drugs, committed an uncountable number of larcenies, burglaries, assaults, and shootings, and victimized scores of innocent people. And for the whole of that time, David never gave a second thought to the pain he caused or the damage he did. He didn't feel remorseful or guilty or sorry. In fact, apart from a determination to keep doing it, he didn't feel anything at all.

In an unforgiving society, we are told that someone who can be so callous for so long is broken beyond repair. There are psychologists who affix a label to people who have lived as David did: "The classic thinking about the sociopathic personality is ... that they do acts against society and ... don't feel remorseful or guilty about what they've done. It's a personality pattern, as opposed to just a short-term problem." "It's a conscienceless kind of person, a person who

* In my interviews, David never admitted to (and I never asked about) involvement in any crimes other than those for which he has already been prosecuted.

doesn't feel bad about doing the wrong thing.... Basically, it's just the way the person is."[9]

3.

In the predawn hours of April 12, 2012, law enforcement descended on David Medina's home on the northwest side of Oklahoma City. Heavily armed officers from the Oklahoma City Gang Task Force were joined by special agents from the FBI and the ATF. Simultaneous raids were conducted against other Juaritos around the city in a coordinated attack aimed at taking down the entire gang. In the end, thirty people were joined in a single indictment. Oklahoma County prosecutors alleged the gang was an ongoing criminal enterprise and charged the defendants with racketeering and conspiracy. David was the lead defendant. He faced a maximum penalty of life imprisonment.

Unlike Richard Rivera, who often said that he had no identity when he was arrested at sixteen, David Medina knew who he was when the cell door slammed behind him. At twenty-eight, he was one of the most important members of one of the largest, most dangerous street gangs in a major US city, a role that had given him everything he had ever wanted: power, respect, money, women. Not many people get to live their childhood dream, but David Medina could honestly say he was living his fantasy life.

But the trappings that accompanied this life—the houses, cars, drugs, and guns; all the *stuff*—were the least important part of his identity. Far more important was the place this identity gave him in the world. An identity gives a person the answers to the questions that everyone eventually asks: Why am I here, who are my people, and how do I create a good life? David knew the answer to these questions: He was here to be the most powerful gangster Oklahoma City had ever known; his people were his family and his fellow

Juaritos; and he created a good life by dominating and eliminating his rivals.

There are barely words in the English language to describe how painful it is to abandon an identity that tells you exactly who you are and where you belong in the world, and to replace it with something entirely foreign. Even the act of recounting the transformation gives events an orderliness that they don't deserve, suggesting that one thing led easily to the next and that the end was never in doubt. But when you are living through it, when you are debating whether to cast off the only way of navigating the world that you have ever known and grasping in the void for something to replace it, the end seems very much in doubt.

Still, there were moments along the way that stand out in David's mind. Even before he was arrested, he had begun to question parts of the life he had long taken for granted. After fifteen years in the gang, which is an entire generation on the street, he no longer felt the need to be so visible, so *present*. He had come a long way from the little boy who rode his bike in the street so all the drivers would see him speeding off to a gang meeting. At the same time, burying so many friends had opened a wound that was increasingly difficult to camouflage as rage, and he began to wonder how many more friends he could stand to lose and how much more pain he would have to endure. And he was tired. He slept with a gun under his pillow, never stayed in the same house two nights in a row, frequently switched the car he drove, and had nothing in his own name, all to stay one step ahead of rival gangs and the police. No one can stay in combat mode forever, and sometimes he just wanted a good night's sleep.

Perhaps all this would have eventually led David away from the gang, but we'll never know because whatever small chink it opened in his armor was quickly hammered shut when he was arrested. In jail, he needed to show that he wasn't afraid of anything or intimidated by anyone. He needed to be the man who laughed at the prosecution's charges and mocked their threats. Jail didn't bother him; he'd been arrested before and had beaten the charges. Once he was taken into custody, he armored up and got ready for war. There was nothing the authorities could do to David Medina. At least, that's what he needed everyone to believe.

But every armor can be pierced. In 2012, David's girlfriend, Cindy, was pregnant with their daughter, Natalie. During the pregnancy, doctors detected a problem with Natalie's heart, and Cindy and her baby had to endure a seemingly endless series of surgeries and treatments. Through it all, David had been by their side. Cindy had another appointment scheduled for April 12, 2012, and David planned to be there, as he always was. But that was the day police raided his home and took him into custody. It was the first appointment he had ever missed. Natalie was born while David was in jail.

And then it happened. David had been charged in both state and federal court, and Natalie died while he languished in a federal jail cell. She was barely a year old. Her death hurled David into a ring of hell where nothing exists but wave after wave of unending torment. It was a wrenching, howling grief that no parent should endure. Courts sometimes let pretrial detainees out of custody so they can attend a family funeral, and David asked the court to let him out so he could bury his daughter. The court refused. He was furious. He tried, as he had when his friends were killed, to conceal his grief with anger and said he "acted the fool," meaning he was as disruptive and as violent as he could possibly be within the confines of a small, steel cell. He banged the doors, beat the walls, cussed the guards, and screamed in the night. But none of that was remotely enough to hide the pain, and in the end, David—like Lucas Whaley—found himself in the most dangerous place in any jail:

alone in his cell with his memories and his loss, overwhelmed by a misery he had never experienced before.

While his grief was still at its worst, David was transferred from federal custody to the Oklahoma County Jail to face the state racketeering charges, where he was held under conditions the likes of which I've never heard before. From his description, it sounds as though he was brought to a single-occupancy holding cell on the first floor of the jail that was intended only for short-term stays. His cell was about the size of a small parking spot, with no natural light and no shower. It had a steel bed, a steel sink, a steel toilet, and a steel slab that functioned as a desk, and that's all. Apart from the guards who delivered meals three times a day through a trap in the door, he had no human contact. I asked him how he showered. "In the sink," he said. People inside call it a birdbath.

For about four months, David never left his cell. Even at the federal super-maximum-security prison in Florence, Colorado, which is the most secure and most restrictive prison the United States has ever built, prisoners are allowed out of their cells about ten hours a week to shower and exercise. And at Florence, they are allowed to see the natural light. David's cell had a narrow slit in the door that looked out into a hallway. Eventually, he was allowed out of his cell once a day, shackled, to pace the hallway or use a shower down the hall. But he still never saw the sun or the natural light. He lived in that cell for four years.

I don't know if Oklahoma County deliberately put David in these conditions or whether he slipped through the bureaucratic cracks (which happens more than you might think), but those conditions created a degree of isolation far more severe than anything routinely practiced in the United States today. They're also clearly unconstitutional. The only thing that comes close, at least in recent memory, are the post-9/11 detentions of CIA prisoners in secret foreign black sites, where the United States government claimed the Constitution didn't apply.* And the reason why the Constitution forbids this kind of treatment—why it is considered cruel and unusual punishment—is because it exacts a horrible physical and mental toll, as it did for David.

It was in this cell that the nightmares overtook him. He had had occasional nightmares while he was in federal custody, which began after his daughter died, but they were not particularly unusual or severe. But in the isolation of the Oklahoma County Jail, he began to have the most violent and terrifying nightmares. He described them as, "like, if you would picture horror movies, but you're actually in the midst of it, living and experiencing it, and it feels so surreal." He suffered through these nightmares "every single night. And I never used to drink coffee, never, and I was in that cell, those nightmares were so severe, that's why I started drinking coffee. Because I was scared to go to sleep. And I would look at the bed and I was frightened of it. . . . Like, when I would lay on it, I would get taken to a whole 'nother adventure that just felt so real." He endured these nightmares for about two and a half years. "So think about several years," he said, "count the days, do the multiplication. Every night, those nightmares."

David hadn't told anyone about his nightmares because he thought they would make him look soft. The prosecutors wanted to lock him up for the rest of his life, and he was determined not to show any weakness. But the combination of endless days spent in isolation and countless nights spent in terror, all while grieving for his daughter and girding himself for battle, was taking a horrible toll. He still wore the mask of the cold-hearted gangster, but behind it was a man who was increasingly exhausted in body and spirit. No one can endure this torture forever, and one night, he had the nightmare that broke him.

* I represent Abu Zubaydah, the first prisoner imprisoned and tortured in a CIA black site.

"It was of my little brother, and we was at a place, and I literally seen people come in, and we were fighting our way to get out and they grabbed him, and as I'm trying to fight these people off of me, they're stabbing us. They have chainsaws and all this stuff. And then I see my little brother, they start chopping him in front of me." In the dream, David struggles to get to his brother, "and as somehow I get to him, like, they chopped all his arms, his legs and everything. And so I'm picking him up and trying to grab his arms and legs. I gotta get him to a hospital like, to save his life." The last thing David remembers is running down the street, carrying the pieces of his brother and screaming. "Then I wake up, just crying...crying like it really actually happened."

Later that day, he was allowed out of his cell briefly and called his mother. He didn't go into the call planning to tell her about his nightmares, but "something happened to me...and then just out of the blue, I start crying.... I wasn't planning to, and it just, like bursts out." Because he had never shared his nightmares, because he had always presented himself as the stone-cold gangster whose only response to pain was fury, his mother was shocked when he broke down on the phone. She spoke later with Guillermo, David's younger brother, who was in custody on the same indictment. Guillermo was also a Juarito but had never held the same rank in the gang as David. He had already made the decision to put the gang behind him, had pled guilty to a reduced charge, and was serving his sentence in an Oklahoma prison. Guillermo spoke with another man in prison about David's nightmare, who told him, "David needs to talk to Sally."

4.

Sally Riesenberg is a lay Catholic chaplain who has been visiting and ministering to people in the Oklahoma County Jail for decades. She has an almost supernatural ability to set people at ease, and to comfort them when they most need comforting. She didn't know anything about David, but, as she would with anyone else, when she learned that someone needed to see her, she agreed to visit him. Her first visit was at David's cell, a few days after David's call with his mother.

David had no idea she was coming and didn't trust her. As he explained to me, "When you're incarcerated, from my experience, when you don't request a chaplain, and a chaplain comes to see you it's because they're about to tell you one of your family members passed away." When he realized Sally wasn't there to give him bad news, he thought it some kind of trick. "So then my second thought was, she's an FBI agent. They're trying to get me to confess." That put David especially on his guard, and he didn't say much as Sally tried to get him to open up. He was respectful, but offered little more of himself than pleasantries and generalities.

But at the end of her visit, "I agreed to something that I didn't know was going to change me. Before she left, she asked me, 'Can I pray for you?' I was like, 'Yeah.'" David paused for a second as he was talking to me, then added, "That was the last night I had nightmares. That was the last night I had those tormenting nightmares."

David believes God reached him that day and brought him peace because he finally opened himself up to His love. He said, "For so long, it's like I wasn't allowing myself to be ready for it." People had tried to reach out to him before and bring him to God, "and I would immediately like, you know what I mean, no, I'm not hearing that. No, no, no. I'm not gonna agree with that. I'm not even thinking of that. . . . I have what I guess you can call a numb, cold heart at the time." But the combination of his daughter's death and the unrelenting nightmares "kind of brought my guard down," and he had taken his armor off without "even realizing it." When Sally asked if she could pray for him, he was at last ready to take the leap of faith.

Still, anyone hoping for a storybook ending, as though the light went on over David's head and, after one good night's sleep, he could finally see the world through completely different eyes, doesn't understand what it means to cast off lifelong habits of mind. Sally visited him nearly every week for eighteen months, and the shift in his thinking was painfully slow. Particularly in the beginning, it was not at all clear that he would turn away from the gang. Early in their relationship, Sally asked David whether he was reading, and when he said he was, she started bringing him magazines and books, including the Bible. "I love reading," David told me, "but it was books that I was studying to do bad things, like, you know, for example, *48 Laws of Power*, *Art of Seduction*, *Art of War*. Books that I could use it to my benefit in a bad way." Sally's books were nothing like these, of course. "I would open up a page and oh my goodness... I would have to shut it. I couldn't get nothing from it. I couldn't read it."

Once again, the way forward came to him in a dream. "I have a dream of my daughter.... This is when *Transformers* was like, a big thing with kids," and in his dream, his daughter wanted David to take her to a *Transformers* movie. "And so I'm driving, and then as I'm driving, I'm happy like, 'My daughter wants to see this movie? I'm going'... And so, it's like it was really happening in real life. I'm driving, heading to the movies, and she starts crying uncontrollably." In the dream, David wonders whether his daughter saw something that upset her. "And then I'm like, 'we're almost at the movies,' and she's like, 'No, Daddy. I want to see that in your life.' I'm like, 'See what in my life?' She's like, 'transformer, transformation.'" That's when he woke up, and "out of the blue, I just got this urge to, like, open up the Bible." David said that's when the process of change truly began.

Slowly, thoughts of a different life would creep into his head, "thoughts I've never had, like, 'What about a change?' About something good, you know what I mean, about something else?" But David "wrestled" with these thoughts, "trying to fight them off" until his mind was thoroughly at war with itself. In time, these competing visions spilled out in the most remarkable way. After the period of intense isolation was over, David was allowed to have magazines in his cell. Some came from Sally, some from other people. Without conscious thought for what he was doing or why, he used to tear pictures from the magazines and affix them to the door of his cell.

Before long, he noticed that the left side of the door was covered "with so much darkness...like, anything you could imagine, like death, darkness and evilness," while on the right side of his door, he pasted pictures of "just beautiful stuff, nature, beautiful colors." On the left were skeletons; on the right, pictures of the ocean. (I asked him how he attached the pictures to his door. "Toothpaste," he said.) A small, metal piece of the door divided the two halves and seemed in David's mind to be a bridge from the left side to the right, "and I'm in a war to get to that." He said his mind was torn, "like, 'you're not supposed to see that, you're not supposed to feel that.' And but then a part of me yearns for that. A part of me wants something that I've never known about."

No mind can be at war with itself forever, and in time, David moved to the light. In making the move, he had help from an unexpected source. Oklahoma is a deeply religious state, and a great many Oklahomans recognize the transformative power of religious conversion. Because Sally has been visiting and ministering to people in the jail for so long, she is well known and trusted by the guards and officers. This worked to David's benefit, and the staff began to believe in David because they believed in Sally and trusted her judgment. In time, the guards started to relax David's conditions of confinement in order to facilitate Sally's visits. They opened his door and allowed Sally to visit with him alone in his cell. Other times, guards joined in Sally's Bible classes, sitting just outside the cell door, participating in the discussion of particular verses, and holding David's hand during prayers. This not only encouraged David's transformation; it also expanded the circle of people who believed in him and his future.

Yet even as he increasingly thought of himself as a child of God, David told me there was no point in his incarceration when the struggle ended completely. At one point, his lawyers offered to get him something to ease his conditions. They expected him to ask for a television or a radio, or perhaps more time out of his cell. David surprised them. "I'd like a chair." Sally only visited once a week, and David needed a way to work through the maelstrom of new ideas roiling his brain. He wanted to write, but that was nearly impossible while he was sitting on his bed, leaning uncomfortably to use the metal slab that passed for a desk. His lawyers convinced the guards to bring him a chair, and in it he wrote poetry for hours.

Academics have devoted surprisingly little time to remorse, perhaps because it's hard to study it ethically. You can't very well create an experiment that induces people to commit a terrible wrong just so you can ask them how they feel about it afterward. To help me make sense of it all, I reached out to Abby Mendelson. Abby is a volunteer chaplain for the Aleph Institute, a Jewish nonprofit that works with people who are isolated from their regular community, including prisoners. For more than twenty years, Abby has served the needs of people inside the walls of minimum-, medium- and maximum-security jails and prisons in West Virginia and Pennsylvania. Because he's been at it for so long, he has seen some people for decades. If there's one thing Abby understands, it's change in a person's moral outlook.

He told me he has seen many people in prison, "especially those who were previously involved with drugs, who have come to a greater religious observance, and who come to the position, 'It wasn't me. I am someone entirely different, and whatever I did then, I would never do now.'" Abby said this is "a form of remorse, and perhaps all that most people can reach." But then he added something else. He said "there is an additional level, a deeper level, that acknowledges, 'That *was* me. I'm responsible for that pain. I'm responsible for that destruction. Me. I did it, and I have to live with it. I have to make it right.'" That, he said, is far more difficult. Abby called it "soul-crushing."

David is in this latter category. In 2016, prosecutors dismissed the racketeering charges against him, and he pled guilty to the distribution of narcotics. He was sentenced to ten to twenty years in prison, ten of which were suspended. He was given credit for the four-plus years he had already spent in state and federal custody and paroled from prison after another eighteen months. In the end, he served a little more than five and a half years, a remarkable resolution that would not have been possible had he not traveled the hard road in the Oklahoma County Jail.

After he was released in 2017, David began establishing the ordinary life he never had before. Though he was nearly thirty-five years old by that time, he'd never had a bank account in his own name, never been employed in the lawful economy, and had no credit history. He'd never had his own name on a rental, let alone a mortgage. He'd never even had a driver's license. Today, he is married and owns his own business pouring concrete at residential and commercial sites around Oklahoma. He is justly proud of his work and the stability it has given him, and takes special joy in the simplest of life's pleasures, like sleeping through the night without a gun under his pillow and enjoying a morning cup of coffee in his backyard, listening to the birds.

But his real passion is his volunteer work. David has become an ordained minister. In 2019, he formed a nonprofit with a group of other former gang members, some of whom used to be in rival gangs. There was a time they shot at each other; now they work together. They travel throughout Oklahoma City—to the county jail and the juvenile detention center, to the people they used to battle and the neighborhoods they used to terrorize. They are looking for themselves, the people they were twenty years ago, when all they knew was violence and all they could express was rage. He said, "That's the ones that want something else. They want out of it. They just don't know how. They don't know how to say it. They don't know how to express it. And that's their inside battle of crying out. They're crying out, but they don't know it." They call their nonprofit Bangin 4 Jesus.

Because some people cannot hear what he has to say, David has learned to listen more than he speaks. He recalls when he was in jail and began to take an interest in the spiritual journey of other Juaritos in the jail. It's not that he wanted to proselytize so much as bring them the calm and serenity he had begun to feel. He couldn't travel around the jail to visit with anyone, so he asked orderlies to be his eyes and ears. Orderlies are inmates who deliver mail or commissary items to people who can't leave their cells. Their access to the entire jail means they become roving whisperers, surreptitiously passing plans and messages throughout the facility. David asked the orderlies to pose specific questions to particular people, and when the orderlies later passed along their response, he knew where they were on their own journey. Sometimes, their answer told him it was time for Sally to include a new person on her rounds. Other times, he could tell it wasn't yet the right moment. "He's not ready," he would tell Sally of someone on another tier. But their time would come, and when it did, David would be there for them.

CHAPTER 7

"HE IS NOT THAT PERSON TODAY"

> At some point after Sarah and Ben went to bed, Dorsey took a single-shot shotgun from the garage and fatally shot Sarah in the jaw from a distance of approximately 12 inches. Dorsey emptied the chamber, reloaded the gun, pressed it against Ben's right ear and shot. Ben died. Dorsey then engaged in sexual intercourse with Sarah's body. After killing Sarah and Ben, Dorsey took Sarah's social security card from a wallet and scattered the contents of the wallet next to her body. He stole various items of personal property from the home and poured bleach on Sarah's torso, genitals and thighs. Dorsey left the home in Sarah's vehicle, drove to Jefferson City and met with a woman from whom he had borrowed money to buy drugs. Dorsey tried to pay the woman with items later determined to belong to Sarah and Ben.
>
> —*STATE V. BRIAN DORSEY*, 318 S.W.3d 648, 650 (Mo. 2010)

> We are all active and former correctional officers and staff at Potosi Correctional Center. We are part of the law enforcement community who believe in law and order. Generally, we believe in the use of capital punishment. But we are in agreement that the death penalty is not the appropriate punishment for Brian Dorsey... We know that he was convicted of murder, but that is not the Brian Dorsey that we know. We urge you, Governor, to exercise your authority under the

> Missouri Constitution to commute Brian's sentence to life in prison without the possibility of parole.
>
> —Letter signed by more than seventy correctional officers and prison staff in support of Brian Dorsey (2024)

1.

As you make your way down a two-lane country road in rural Missouri, about an hour and a half southwest of St. Louis, it's easy to spot the home of Ralph and Carolyn Curtis. Just look for the wall of flags that line the front yard. There's "Back the Blue," a black-and-white version of the Stars and Stripes that honors fallen police officers; "Don't Tread on Me," the yellow, colonial-era flag with the distinctive coiled rattlesnake that stands for individual liberty and resistance to an oppressive government; the scarlet and gold flag of the United States Marine Corps; and a bunch of flags in support of Donald Trump. There's about ten in all, with an American flag smack in the middle of the yard. Ralph and Carolyn, who have been married more than half a century, finish each other's sentences, and when I asked about the flags, Ralph said he started putting them up in 2020, and Carolyn jumped in to explain the timing: "When Joe took office. When they cheated Trump out of his office."

Their ranch house sits well back from the road, with a broad front yard that slopes gently down to the street. Their home has a much-loved, much-lived feel to it, with a joyful clutter that starts on the counters, spreads to the kitchen, and flows easily into the living room, where the couch looks as though it has been a trusted family friend for many years. Everything about their home puts you at ease, and you feel like you could pull up a chair, pour a cup of coffee, and spend the better part of the day settling the fate of the universe. We were sitting at their kitchen table. Carolyn sat across from me, her arms folded in front of her, and Ralph was on my left, leaning in with one forearm resting on the table. Roxy, a small dog of mixed breed and great energy, padded around at our feet. Carolyn had baked an assortment of cookies.

We were talking about their combined half century at Potosi, the maximum-security prison not far from where they live. Ralph was with Potosi from its earliest days, beginning as a correctional officer. "I went over there in '88, and they didn't even have the fences up or anything yet." He had been working at Farmington Correctional Center twenty-five miles away, and the Department of Corrections sent him to Potosi to provide security. "In January of '89, they finally opened the prison up." The official line is that Potosi was built to hold about 950 inmates, but Ralph recalls it differently. "It was originally for 500, but they double-bunked all the cells." Before long, he shifted to the civilian side and worked in the warehouse and the commissary, managing the constant flow of deliveries into and out of the prison.

Ralph used to work with a number of other civilians, but that gradually changed. "Every year, if something happened to where one of the storekeepers quit, they wouldn't hire another one back. So it ended up, I was the only [civilian] working in the warehouse, and there was one person in the canteen. They just went crazy trying to cut back and save money." "That's the Missouri way," Carolyn added. She joined Potosi shortly after Ralph and was a correctional officer for twenty-two years. She worked just about everywhere in the prison, beginning as the lone officer in the tower that looms over the facility, armed with an AK-47 and instructions to make sure no one got over the fence. On her last tour, she was a sergeant in the control center, "but before that, I was the only rec officer [in the yard]. They would release the inmates, and 200 of them could come out on the rec yard. And I was the only officer out on the outer rec yard."

Understaffing like this is not unique to Missouri. Prisons all over the country save millions of dollars every year by using prison labor. Civilians and correctional officers who work in prisons in this country are notoriously underpaid, but they make a lot more than inmates doing the same job, especially when you add in the cost of benefits, insurance, and social security. States are only too happy to cut that expense. A survey by the Department of Justice in 1990 found that fourteen states even used prisoners to build new prisons.[1]

If there's a silver lining to this penny-pinching, it's that in many parts of the country, the people who can't go home at night live and work shoulder to shoulder with the people who can, sometimes for years at a time. You can get to know a person pretty well in that time. Carolyn said, "You can't be around people on a five day a week basis, eight hours, forty hours a week, without developing a relationship with a person."

2.

No little boy lies awake at night thinking, "When I grow up, I want to be an addict. I want to steal from everyone I know, lie to everyone who loves me, wreck every relationship I'm in, and blow every chance I get." And no little boy thinks how cool it would be to grow up and become mentally ill. To be so depressed he can't get out of bed. So depressed he thinks he doesn't deserve to be loved. But that's the life that some children have.

By all accounts, Brian Dorsey's parents loved him very much, as did his large extended family. But sometimes, a loving and supportive family isn't enough. Brian's father was an alcoholic, as were several of his aunts, uncles, and cousins on both sides of the family. A few more were addicted to pain pills or cocaine or methamphetamines. A cousin took his own life by huffing paint when he was only sixteen, but not before he tried to burn his mother's house down because "the voices" told him to. Brian's parents also suffered from depression, as did several of his cousins. A fistful of aunts and uncles were under psychiatric care for anxiety or depression, and another cousin was on Social Security disability because of her mental health problems.

Brian's father was an unhappy alcoholic who was distant when he was sober and mean when he was drunk. Brian grew up to the sound of his parents fighting and his mother screaming. When he was eleven, he was hospitalized with stomach pains that wouldn't quit. Years later, when an investigator asked his mother to describe what life was like with her husband, she hinted at the sad life of her lonely child. She described her husband as "a very belligerent alcoholic" and "always very negative." Of homelife, she said, "We walked around on eggshells" and "Brian could never do anything right." He "spent a lot of time in his room."

For some children, the waters just seem to part. You can always spot them, wearing the right clothes and drinking in the envy of others. Brian never set foot in those circles. He was never the popular one in school and didn't come from money. The classroom was just that place he went every day to be humiliated. There were no younger siblings to worship him as cool, and no older ones to whisk him past the invisible velvet ropes that separate winners from losers in every school in the country. He was big for his age, which landed him a spot on the high school football team, but he wasn't athletic or flashy and never played the glamour positions. He was the thick-necked lineman who got his bell rung on just about every play. At his trial many years later, his coach said Brian was "maybe not the greatest talent in the world," but he "played as hard as he could." He dropped out of high school after his senior season. He was seventeen.

But Brian Dorsey had one thing going for him. *Lovable*—that's the word that comes up again and again in the recollection of cousins who grew up with him. As one cousin said, "I cannot ever remember seeing Brian fight. The meanest thing Brian ever did to me was hug me too tightly." His football coach used to call him Chumley, after the dim-witted walrus with a big belly and a bigger heart in the *Tennessee Tuxedo* cartoons. Nobody could remember him raising a hand against another soul. When a cousin heard the police were looking for him in connection with a double murder, "it literally knocked the wind out of me." The day he turned himself in was the first and only time his name had been connected to violence.

But *lovable* is not the same as *happy*. If you tell a little boy he's stupid and worthless—that he doesn't have the brains of a goat and will never amount to anything—he'll come to believe it. In time, he'll see the world through the eyes you've given him. Every failed test proves he's a moron. Every casual slight confirms he'll always be alone. Every setback reminds him he's a failure. Pretty soon he stops trying because who's he kidding? Everybody knows how this movie ends. As the depressed and lonely child of an abusive alcoholic, Brian believed that people would abandon him. He was a people-pleaser, always solicitous of others in the vain hope that they would accept him but always expecting that they would not, and that they would see him for the loser he knew he was. For Brian Dorsey, being lovable was a desperation to be loved.

Brian's mother always knew when the clouds had descended in her son's life because he couldn't get out of bed. Throughout his twenties, Brian often lived in his parents' basement. He'd drag himself upstairs just long enough to eat, then slump back downstairs and collapse into bed, exhausted. Brian started drinking when he was little, but getting drunk didn't become his mission in life until he was fifteen. He'd cajole some cousin to buy him a twelve-pack of beer or a pint of liquor. Alcohol meant a party, and Brian needed parties in his life. To ease the pain of his depression, he went to the bars and drank, which gave him the fleeting illusion that life was fun and that people liked him. He drank nearly every day of his adult life. Booze became his antidepressant.

One day when he was out drinking, a drug dealer in Cedar City, Missouri, introduced Brian to crack cocaine. Crack is a god-awful thing. When you start, it gives you the feeling that the word *euphoria* is meant to describe. And when you live in a world that never feels that way, crack is the friend you can't live without. In the real world, the world where everything sucks and you're clinically depressed, crack is your salvation.

Until it isn't. All that time crack is making your world sunny and bright, it's snaking around your insides, until one day you discover it's settled under your skin, so you can feel it but can't claw it out. Then you realize it's made its way into your head, where it squares off against your brain. Sometimes you win. Sometimes you can still clown around with your cousins and give your mother a bear hug and feel like your old self. But sometimes crack wins. When you've been at a bar drinking and think the good times deserve to be a little better. Or when you're home after another shitty day, and goddamn, wouldn't it be great to have just one hit and feel a little bit like you did that first time?

The more you fight this battle, the worse your odds get. Crack starts to win more rounds until it's winning damn near all the time. Pretty soon, it's not just one hit. It's one after another, for days at a time, until you're nervous and jittery and can't finish a sentence but can't stop talking. It doesn't make you feel smart or funny anymore; it just lets you get through another day. Until you've pawned everything you own and stole all the money you can from all the friends and family who'll still answer your phone calls. Until your money is gone, and your dealer won't front you any more drugs. Until your body collapses.

And you wake up from a binge in a haze of half memories that somehow got you from your bare floor to a broken-down couch in an apartment you don't recognize, surrounded by people you don't know. You can't remember what you did or where you did it, but your microwave is gone and so is your TV. So is your money and your job. All that's left—and it's everywhere—is shame. You hate yourself and just want it all to stop. It's an agony that nothing can touch.

Brian was twenty-one the first time he tried to kill himself. He swallowed a medicine cabinet full of pills and washed it down with cough syrup and beer. His mother found him in the basement, surrounded by empty bottles. In the records from his stay in the hospital, the medical staff reported "he was feeling despondent because he is addicted to Cocaine and he has huge financial problems as a result of this addiction. The patient estimates he spent 800 to 900 dollars just last month on the drug alone. He recently sold his car for cocaine."

When he got out of the hospital, he told himself and his mother that he was going to get his life together. He moved to St. Louis, got his GED, went to barber school, and got a job cutting hair. Turns out he was good at it. His boss liked him. There was talk of Brian taking over the shop. But if you've never suffered from clinical depression, count yourself lucky. No matter how good things seemed to be from the outside, Brian knew that any momentary joy was just a mirage in the desert of his life. When things fell apart, as he knew they would, the pain would be even worse if he had been stupid enough to let himself believe this time would be different. Better to just bring it on now and get it over with. He sabotaged nearly every job he ever had.

And so it went, throughout his twenties. "One failed job after another and one failed relationship after another," Brian later told his lawyers. "I started to become more and more depressed and tired of life treating me bad. I just wanted to be happy and I could never achieve that for very long. Life was never as good as it used to be or like it was supposed to be. I kept getting deeper in the abyss… [s]inking deeper and deeper into the pit. Hating my life… More and more drugs and alcohol to fill that hole inside of me." For a decade, he had a forgettable string of dead-end jobs and part-time hustles. He went to treatment a couple of times for his crack and alcohol addictions, and it helped, at least for a while. He'd stop drinking for a bit, and sometimes he'd hold down a job for a year or so. For a while, he was the lovable son and cousin, with the big hug and ready laugh. But it wasn't treatment for his depression, which was the beast he was trying to escape with all that alcohol and crack, and his mental illness always caught up with him. Then he'd spend his time drinking, just to be around people and to hear the sound of laughter. Then he'd start using again, and then the binging would restart.

You hear people describe it as a cycle. That's what some of Brian's lawyers would eventually say. But that's not right. Photosynthesis is a cycle. Sunrise to sunset and back to sunrise—that's a cycle. But using crack and alcohol to outrun clinical depression is like living with a parasite that kills its host. Your life might look like good days follow bad ones, at least at first. But the longer the parasite lives inside you, the fewer good days you have. Eventually, they're not really good; they're just less bad. It's not a cycle; it's what life looks like when your body and mind are dragged into a hole that light cannot enter. That's how it was for Brian. "The more my life slipped out of my hands, my use got more out of control. I was just living to get high. Make myself feel better and forget life and the guilt, shame of being a failure at everything."

By his early thirties, Brian could no longer hold down a full-time job. He'd work just long enough to earn a few hundred bucks to pay for his next binge. No one knew when the spiral would end, but everyone could see it would end badly. In September 2004, a physician finally put him on antidepressants. Two months later, his wife of fourteen months found him in a crack house in Jefferson City, Missouri. He hadn't eaten or slept for days and later told her he "was going to do drugs till he died." When he left the crack house, he was arrested and charged with possession of crack. Two months after that, he was arrested again, this time at a different crack house. Neither of the charges put a dent in his crack habit. He was thirty-two.

In May 2005, he stole money from one of his cousins to buy crack, and when the binge ended, he pummeled himself with guilt. He tried again to kill himself, this time by overdosing on his antidepressants. Back in the hospital, he told the staff he'd been depressed for more than a decade. In hospital records, the nurses distilled his misery to "helplessness, hopelessness, worthlessness, and suicidal thoughts." When the staff asked him his chief complaint, he said, "things are falling apart."

Some might say that Brian surrendered to his addiction, but that's not right. Like a man hanging from a ledge, he never let himself go. Time and again, he tried to climb back to solid ground, and time and again, it seemed as though he might. He'd clean himself up, get a job, and move into a new place. Once again, he'd be the lovable oaf, the family clown, asking after others and making fun of himself. Maybe this time, his sobriety would hold. Family and friends allowed themselves the illusion of hope. He didn't want to disappoint everyone who loved him and betray everyone who trusted him, and he hated himself when he did. He wanted desperately to change and struggled to control his addiction and overcome his depression. But the longer he fought the battle, the weaker he became, and as his strength gradually collapsed, his shame grew deeper.

In December 2005, thoughts of suicide brought him back to the hospital. He said he'd "been depressed for several years running," but that lately his depression had gotten even worse. The medical staff reported he was "feeling guilt, and blaming himself," with "visions of hanging himself or cutting his wrists." He told them he was "tired of living." He was hospitalized five days and felt pretty good when he left. But two days later, an ambulance brought him back. Seems he ran into some friends after he was discharged, and they asked him over to watch football. As the hospital staff would later report, "he agreed to go and then agreed to go have a beer, which led to more and then led to him going out looking [and finding] crack cocaine, which he smoked until 10 am the next day. Brian then felt guilty and worthless . . . Later that day, after drinking and drugging all night and no sleep, he slit his wrist." "I'm tired of hurting," he said.

In January 2006, he was finally added to the waiting list for inpatient mental health and substance abuse treatment. He was still on that list when he was arrested for murder almost twelve months later. In April, he picked up a new felony. He had split with his wife and was driving with his girlfriend on his lap, she as drunk as he. He slammed into another car and fled before the police arrived. He was arrested a week later and charged with fleeing the scene of an accident. In June, he pled guilty to two possession charges and promised the judge he'd stay clean and sober for five years—just another promise he wanted to keep, but suspected he'd break. In September, he pled guilty to the fleeing charge and got five more years of probation. He worked a few days that year. Even managed to report a few times to his probation officer and provide clean urine samples. But he spent most of the year chasing after a white powder that had been dissolved in water, cut with baking soda, boiled to a solid, and chipped into rocks.

3.

Prison changes everyone, but sometimes not in the way they expect. On his first day at Potosi, Ralph said he thought he'd be surrounded by "all these hard and, you know—" Carolyn jumped in to finish the thought, "bad, ugly men." "It wasn't what I was expecting," Ralph told me. "I was expecting, you know, all these, just hard ass people." Carolyn became animated when she talked about the difference between myth and reality. Those who don't know any better think people in prison "are just born killers. No, they're not."

I tried to get at how and why Ralph and Carolyn's views had changed. But for them, it wasn't a very important question; their views changed because they saw the world for what it is, rather than what they had imagined it to be, and when myth smacks into reality, only the willfully blind hold onto old ways of thinking. Carolyn said, "I thought when you went to work at the prison, you were against the inmates and staff always had your back. That's not true. I had more inmates that had my back than staff."

One day, she was the lone CO in the outer yard when a man named William Weaver sidled up and began chatting with her about this or that. While Weaver distracted her, two other inmates squared off in a knife fight in a far corner of the yard. This was a bold act on Weaver's part: If he hadn't drawn Carolyn's attention away, she would've been expected to break up the fight by putting herself between the two fighters, at great personal risk. By keeping her out of harm's way, Weaver was breaking an unwritten rule by protecting a CO.

Yet Weaver was doing what he knew was right. Months earlier, Ralph had saved Weaver's life after he had been stabbed. Saving Carolyn was Weaver's way of repaying a debt that transcended the unwritten rules of the yard. When Carolyn discovered the fight was going on, she hollered at Weaver for distracting her. But Weaver was unfazed. "Weaver looked at me, and he goes, 'There ain't no way in H that I'm gonna look Ralph Curtis in the eye and tell him why I didn't protect you after he saved my life. Get mad all you want, but that's the way it is out here.'" At the time, Weaver was on death row. His death sentence was eventually set aside because of prosecutorial misconduct. Weaver is now serving a life sentence.

Still, I think Ralph and Carolyn are being too modest. The fact is that a lot of people can stare reality in the face and still cling to myth. I think they were willing to reconsider their ideas about prison because they know, just as sure as I was sitting with them at their kitchen table on a hot Missouri morning, that under different circumstances, it could've been them in prison. "I did crap when I was younger," Ralph said, "and other than for the grace of God, that could be me."

And for Carolyn, it nearly was. One afternoon, a young man came to their door, in tears. I'll call him James, though that's not his real name. James was a friend of Carolyn's teenage son, who was thirteen or fourteen at the time, and he told Carolyn that the man her son was working for was a pedophile who abused teenage boys. James knew this because he had been one of the man's victims years earlier. James told Carolyn the man "would take these young boys into his trailer with pornography magazines and feed them beer." He had molested James for years, but James had been too ashamed to tell anyone. But now he was bringing it into the open because he was afraid the same thing would happen to Carolyn's son.

Carolyn was beside herself with rage. She immediately told James to report the man to the police but had no intention of waiting for them to act. "I loaded the gun. As soon as he left, I loaded the gun to go kill" the man. She set the rifle in the back seat of her car and was about to leave when her daughter pulled into the driveway behind her, blocking her exit from the garage. Her daughter could tell immediately that Carolyn was furious about something. She said, "Mom, what are you doing with that rifle?" Carolyn told her, "I gotta go take care of some business." Her daughter became alarmed. "She goes, 'Tell me what's going on.'" Carolyn relayed what James had said and told her daughter to move her car and get out of the way. Her daughter refused and frantically called Ralph, who raced home from work and managed to talk Carolyn out of her homicidal plan.

But Carolyn has no doubt about what she would've done. "I'd have killed him." And she knows what probably would've happened. "If I had made it to his house with that .30-06, I probably would've gotten life. Or the death penalty." She's probably right, since it turns out the man had not abused her son, though he had abused several other boys and was eventually sent to prison. But at the time, she was not in a mind to wait for these details. When we spoke, many years after it had all taken place, I asked her if she really meant what she was saying. "So be honest with yourself now," I said. "Literally, if she hadn't been parked behind you—" She cut me off. "He'd have been dead. I'd have killed him. So, that's why, I don't *condone* murder. I *understand* murder."

4.

At his trial, Brian testified he'd been up two or three days, drinking and smoking crack. But then he was broke and he owed his dealer money. He started calling cousins, begging them for $150. Then his dealer showed up at his apartment with an enforcer. She demanded to be paid and refused to leave. One of Brian's cousins came over with her husband. Another cousin joined them, along with her husband. The four of them convinced the dealer and her associate to leave. While his family was rescuing him, Brian sat on the couch, sobbing. He was embarrassed and humiliated. The group then went to the home of one of his cousins, Sarah Bonnie, where they started drinking. They drank for hours. It was Christmas Eve, 2006.

Brian told the jury he couldn't remember everything that happened once the drinking stopped and people staggered off to sleep. He hadn't slept for days and had done a lot of coke and drunk a lot of alcohol. He remembers being in Sarah's bedroom. He remembers having the shotgun and remembers thinking he would use it to kill himself. But he didn't remember shooting her, or her husband, Ben.

He didn't remember having sex with Sarah's dead body, and can't believe he could possibly have done that.* He didn't remember stealing their car and a bunch of their stuff, and could only vaguely recall being in some apartment somewhere, trying to sell it so he could buy more crack. But Brian never denied that he was responsible for their deaths, and he hated himself for it. When he thought about what he had done, it filled him with a visceral feeling of disgust. He knew the police were looking for him and turned himself in the day after Christmas. He pled guilty to capital murder and a Missouri jury sentenced him to die.

5.

It took seventeen years for Brian's case to lumber through state and federal court. His appeals were denied, and when Missouri finally decided it was time to kill him, an investigator who worked with his lawyers reached out to Ralph and Carolyn Curtis. "He got us talking about Brian," and when they were done reminiscing, he asked whether they would sign a letter on Brian's behalf. They agreed. The one-page letter, which asked the governor to commute Brian's sentence to life imprisonment, was eventually signed by more than seventy current and former correctional officers and prison staff.

I asked Ralph and Carolyn if signing the letter had been a difficult decision. "It wasn't hard," Carolyn said. "We both knew Brian and felt pretty good about what we were saying." Maybe that shouldn't have surprised me, but the fact is that prison staff almost never sign letters in support of inmates, and certainly not inmates scheduled to be executed. I thought maybe they were just opposed to capital punishment.

---

* Though the prosecution argued that Brian had sex with his cousin's body after she had been killed, the evidence was disputed and he was not charged with sexual assault.

No, that wasn't it. Like many people, they have problems with the way the death penalty is administered in this country—Carolyn said she "always felt the death penalty has never been handed out justly. If you're poor and have a public defender, you're going to get the death penalty, but if you have money, you'll get life"—but they accept it in some cases, and Ralph mentioned in particular the murder of a police officer or the rape and murder of a child.

Then I thought that perhaps they didn't know what Brian had done. I read them the paragraph from the Missouri Supreme Court that I quote at the beginning of this chapter. They were silent after I finished, which made me realize they hadn't heard these facts before. "It sounds pretty heinous when you read it all at once like that," Carolyn said. I asked if they would've signed the letter if they had known these facts at the time. They paused again, but this time only for an instant. Yes, Carolyn said, they would've done it all over again "because we spent twenty years with him."

As his execution date approached, Brian's lawyers put together a packet of information for the governor of Missouri. The first thing they highlighted was the letter from the COs and prison staff. But they also told the governor all the things that lawyers say at times like this. Brian never got a disciplinary ticket in prison, which is extraordinary. As Ralph said, "it's *really* hard to go without any violations. Even the most chill inmate gets *some* violations." That's especially true at Potosi. In most states, death row inmates are kept in solitary confinement nearly twenty-four hours a day. But in Missouri, people on the row are part of the general population.[2] They can participate in programming, learn a trade, and have a job. Yet because it's such a high-security prison, Potosi is the place where the Department of Corrections (DOC) sends its problems. As the former warden there once explained, "when offenders throughout the state exhibit extreme acts of inappropriate behavior," the DOC is likely to ship them to

Potosi. In a place like that, it's easy to become a target or get swept into the chaos. Brian never did. The lawyers also pointed out that for the last twelve years or so, Brian had been the staff barber at Potosi, and you don't get that job unless the COs trust you enough to stand behind them with a razor. And they said that Brian had lived in the Honors Dorm for years, which is reserved for people who follow all the rules.

Ralph and Carolyn knew all this, but I didn't get the feeling it made all that much difference to them. Yes, they knew Brian was the staff barber because he cut Ralph's hair every two weeks. Yes, they knew where he lived because Carolyn had been a CO in the Honors Dorm. Yes, they assumed he never got a violation because he never made trouble. But when I talked with them, it just didn't seem as though they had all that in mind when they decided to sign the letter to the governor. What was important to the lawyers just wasn't that important to them. I had trouble figuring out their reasoning until I went back to the one-page letter and noticed a sentence I had skipped over before: "Brian is a good guy." When I first read that, I thought it was just a throwaway line and didn't pay it much attention. But they said it twice. In fact, in the whole letter, it was the only sentiment that appears more than once. Elsewhere, they wrote, "There isn't a nicer guy than Brian." Brian Dorsey killed his cousin and her husband, then allegedly sexually assaulted his cousin's dead body, but more than six dozen correctional officers and prison staff at a maximum-security prison were describing him as a good guy.

Then something made me think back to Klete Keller, the Olympic swimmer whose former teammates and coaches pleaded on the front page of the *New York Times* that he not be judged too harshly for his role in the insurrection at the US Capitol on January 6, 2021. I remembered a line that one of his teammates used to describe Keller: "Great person, great soul, great teammate." They also supplied an explanation for Keller's behavior that softened his culpability. As one former coach said, Keller was just "at the wrong place, at the wrong time, with the wrong people."

These people were not asking that Keller be excused; they knew he had to be held accountable for what he had done. Instead, they were pleading that he be judged not as a monster, but as one of us, as someone who strayed as any of us might stray. They were asking that society judge him in a spirit of forgiveness. They were making a plea for social forgiveness because they knew him as a human being, that cauldron of contradictions, ugly and kind in the same soul.

Though Brian's crime was immeasurably more serious than Keller's, the more than seventy correctional officers and prison staff were making precisely the same plea in their letter. While I was writing this chapter, I spoke with Matt Frierdich, Brian's spiritual advisor. Once Missouri scheduled Brian's execution, the prison allowed Matt extra time to meet with him, so Matt spent a great deal of time with Brian in the months before his scheduled execution. This gave him a unique opportunity to watch Brian's interactions with COs and staff. Matt told me he was struck by the convivial plainness of it. Brian was everyone's pal, cracking jokes, asking after their kids and swapping stories about the game on TV the previous night. Brian knew everyone and everyone knew him; their interactions had the unmistakable effortlessness that can only be described as friendship.

The COs and staff had lived with Brian half his adult life and had come to know him as a human being, and not as a story in the newspapers. Like Keller's coaches, they supplied an explanation that allowed them to make sense of behavior that otherwise seemed incomprehensible. As one CO put it in a separate letter, "I believe that Brian must have been extremely high on drugs and out of his mind to have committed murder or even to have caused harm to another person. He is not that person today." Another officer in a letter said,

"If you ask me, if it were not for drugs, none of this would've happened. The Mr. Dorsey I know must have been out of his mind at the time this happened." Or as Ralph Curtis said when we spoke, "if he'd have been sober, I don't think he would've done it."

Which, of course, is what his family always knew and had been trying to explain. Shortly before his scheduled execution, one of Brian's cousins lamented, "I wish someone, a decision maker, could see Brian for who he is when not on drugs; he is that person today."[3] None of them were saying that Brian should escape responsibility; their letters asked only that the governor commute Brian's sentence to life in prison, and when we spoke, Ralph and Carolyn made it clear that Brian had to be punished for what he did, and they thought he should never be released. Instead, they were asking that Brian be judged in the same spirit of forgiveness as Keller—not as part of a mythical "them," but as one of us, and that he be allowed to live out his days, as Carolyn put it, "as a responsible human being."

Missouri Governor Mike Parson rejected their plea. In a press release announcing his decision, Parson said, "Brian Dorsey punished his loving family for helping him in a time of need. His cousins invited him into their home where he was surrounded by family and friends, then gave him a place to stay. Dorsey repaid them with cruelty, inhumane violence, and murder."[4] Brian was executed by the State of Missouri April 9, 2024.

CHAPTER 8

THE WHATABOUTS

> The record clearly supports the plaintiffs' argument that the defendants' conduct was intentional and malicious, and certain to cause harm by virtue of their infrastructure, ability to spread content, and massive audience including the "infowarriors." The record also establishes that the defendants repeated the conduct and attacks on the plaintiffs for nearly a decade, including during the trial, wanton, malicious, and heinous conduct that caused harm to the plaintiffs. This depravity, and cruel, persistent course of conduct by the defendants establishes the highest degree of reprehensibility and blameworthiness.
>
> —*ERICA LAFFERTY V. ALEX EMRIC JONES*, Opinion Upholding Punitive Damages, No. X06-UWY-CV18-6046436-S (Superior Court, Complex Litigation Docket, Waterbury, Connecticut, November 10, 2022)

When people learn that I believe American society is inexcusably unforgiving and that I am writing a book that invites us to see the world with different eyes, I get two reactions, often from the same person. The first is enthusiastic agreement. "Yes!" they say. "We're *so* unforgiving. It's terrible." It seems everyone knows of someone who has been treated with undue severity, who has been cast out as the "other." Often, it has happened to them. But then they pause, reflect a moment, and ask, "But what about . . . ?" The whatabouts are the people (or category of people) who have engaged in behavior they find incomprehensibly cruel. As far as they are concerned, if there is an "other," it's the whatabout. For many people, President Trump is a whatabout, as are various people in his orbit. For many others, it's the serial rapist or pedophile. For still others, it's someone like Derek Chauvin, the former Minneapolis police officer who slowly squeezed the life out of George Floyd in May 2020. It seems that everyone has a whatabout, and for a long time, I did too.

For some people, the attachment to the whatabout reflects confusion about what I mean by a forgiving society. I'm not saying that people who cause great pain should escape responsibility for what they did. Derek Chauvin committed a horrible wrong and needs to be held accountable. But everyone I have written about in these pages committed a horrible wrong. If we ask only what they did, the answer is that Lisa Montgomery killed an innocent woman to steal her fetus and raise it as her own child. Eric Matthews beat a helpless child to death. Richard Rivera killed an off-duty police officer who was trying to prevent him from robbing a tavern. Lucas Whaley tortured a man to death and then poured bleach down his throat. Brian Dorsey killed his cousin and her husband while they slept. David Medina was a high-ranking member of a street gang that terrorized Oklahoma City for years. But none of them, including Derek Chauvin, is the "other." All of them did monstrous things, but none of them are monsters. Once we understand what happened, we can see them in us and us in them, and judge them in a spirit of forgiveness.

When I point this out, some people say that I am comparing apples to oranges. Richard raised himself on the streets of New York from the time he was six. Lisa was psychotic and delusional. Eric grew up immersed in neighborhood violence that distorted his thinking. From an early age, Lucas had the shit beaten out of him by a stepfather who mocked everything he loved. And so on. Chauvin, by contrast, was a white police officer who killed an unarmed and defenseless Black man on video, indifferent to the pleas of his victim and bystanders. In short, some people say that Chauvin is more blameworthy because he had opportunities and privileges that many others did not. I have heard this very complaint from some of my students, who one minute enthusiastically embrace my view that there is no them, and the next minute denounce Chauvin as a monster. He is their whatabout.

But of course, my students are prepared to judge Lisa, Eric, Richard, Brian, Lucas, and David in a spirit of forgiveness only because they have learned their stories. They know what happened and can place their crimes in the long arc of lives marked by pain and promise. By contrast, virtually all they know about Chauvin is what they saw on that horrible video. They know what he did, not what happened. And if they close their mind to what happened—if they refuse to consider Chauvin as a complex and flawed human being who did a horrible thing, but who nonetheless has a past behind him and a future before him—then they too have been seduced by the siren song of the unforgiving society.

And yet…

For a long time, my whatabout was Alex Jones. Jones is the enormously popular conspiracy theorist who insisted the mass shooting at Sandy Hook Elementary School was a hoax, that the grief-stricken parents were "actors," and that the whole charade was a plot orchestrated by the federal government to strip people of their guns. He continued to spew his lies even as some of his many followers taunted, tormented, and harassed the grief-stricken parents. His behavior was unspeakably callous. Even after juries awarded roughly one billion dollars in damages to some of the people he victimized, lawyers say he continues to evade responsibility by fraudulently shielding and concealing his assets.[1] To this day, he has not made a serious attempt to atone for the pain he caused. Even as I write these words, I feel the pull of demonization. Sometimes I think, if ever there were a monster, it is him.

But then I remind myself that I know only what he did, not what happened that brought him to this point. The best research suggests that conspiracy theorists tend to have "a sense of antagonism toward others and high levels of paranoia," and that the people most attached to conspiracies, perhaps like Jones, are "insecure, paranoid, emotionally volatile, impulsive, suspicious, withdrawn, manipulative, egocentric and eccentric."[2] Combine these personality traits with an unwavering belief that their in-group is not only superior to all others but continually under threat, and you have the profile of someone predisposed to grasp at outlandish conspiracy theories.[3] Some of them may even act on their paranoia by lashing out at its imagined source, like the Florida woman who sent four death threats to the father of one of the Sandy Hook victims and was later sent to prison.[4] Though their beliefs may lead them to do monstrous things, conspiracy theorists are not monsters. Richard Rivera would say they are just people coping with their world the only way they know how.

Compounding all this is the toxic allure of money and status. I suspect Jones has been consumed by the identity he has made for himself—an identity that has not only given him great wealth but great fame. His conspiratorial rantings and falsehoods have made him a hero to millions of followers, and he basks in their adulation. I imagine it must be irresistibly seductive to be celebrated as a prophet in one's own time. And I imagine how hard it would be for him to look in the mirror and acknowledge that his life is built on lies and gratuitous cruelty. Because most people do not have the strength for that kind of personal reckoning, because they cannot do what David Medina did and shed the identity they painstakingly built for themselves, they continue to live the lie.

Of course, I don't know Jones and don't know if these explanations or something like them are part of his story. But I know there is a story waiting to be uncovered, and that, if he were willing to share that story with the same courage and candor as the people I write about in this book, it would challenge my impulse to cast him out. None of his story would excuse what he did, which was unfathomably cruel, but it would go a long way toward explaining it. More importantly, it would prove, at least to my satisfaction, that he is no more a monster than I am. And, if I am brutally honest with myself, I would admit that, if I traveled in his head and saw the world through his eyes, I could have done what he did. It pains me to write these words, but I could be Alex Jones. I could be the whatabout.

THE WAY FORWARD

I wrote this book because I no longer recognize my own home, and because I think a great many people feel the same way. Like me, they are appalled and repulsed by the cultural celebration of cruelty. They too wish our world were different. But what is the way forward? I have struggled with that question for many years, and this book is my answer. The answer is not a law, and what we seek cannot be converted into a statute or written into the Constitution. The answer is not a judicial decision, and what we seek will not be pronounced by any court. The answer is not an election, and what we hope to build cannot be delivered at the ballot box. The answer is much more simple and infinitely more profound: The answer is to see us in them and them in us. No one is the "other," and no one should be cast out.

This is a book about a place that does not yet exist. But we can become a forgiving society. It requires a new perspective, not a new planet. There was a time when we did not settle our disputes by shooting each other. Yes, the journey to get from here to there will be more difficult than we all might hope. We live in an age when demonization is a first impulse rather than a last resort. Society has become singularly adept at casting out those who we believe have sinned against us. We have become this way because the inclination to treat a fellow human being as irredeemably unworthy of membership is, for many people, irresistibly seductive. It is a temptation that today seduces the left as much as the right, the rich as much as the poor, the young as much as the old. In a world where Americans seem to agree on nothing at all, they agree on this: We are surrounded by monsters.

But we aren't. There is only us, and that is challenge enough.

On January 20, 2025, President Trump pardoned Klete Keller, along with more than 1,500 other people who had been convicted for their role in the riot at the US Capitol four years earlier. As Keller said of the pardon, "Waking up this morning, I was like, 'My gosh. Wow, this is over.' I'm just so grateful that I have the opportunity now to move forward."[1]

ACKNOWLEDGMENTS

It takes a lot of people to bring a book into the world, and I have accumulated a great many debts that I can never repay. To begin with, I am grateful to the many hundreds of people I have met in prisons and jails across the country and around the world, from tiny lockups in rural Minnesota to the federal death row in Terre Haute, Indiana; from a maximum-security prison in Milan to the makeshift cells of Guantánamo Bay and Camp Cropper, Iraq. I am who I am not because of lawsuits I have filed or cases I have argued, not because of books or essays I have written or students I have taught but because of the time I have spent listening to people who lived in a cage.

I am especially indebted to Eric Matthews, Lucas Whaley, Richard Rivera, and David Medina, who spent hours answering my questions and candidly recounting the most painful moments in their life. I marvel at their strength and courage. But I have failed if I have left anyone with the impression that they are heroes. They are not. They are something much more. They have done horrid and wonderful things, and therefore teach us by their example what it means to be human. Listening to them, I often felt that I was being given an invaluable gift. As much as anyone, they are responsible for my personal philosophy, my moral North Star—there is no them, there is only us—and I am grateful to them. (Eric asked me to include that he is particularly grateful to his parents, and to the many people at Angola who wrote on his behalf, for the love and support they showed him throughout his incarceration.)

Lisa Montgomery and Brian Dorsey were executed before I began writing this book, and I regret that I never met them. I know their stories from the Herculean efforts of their advocates, who documented the life their clients had lived. Their work enabled me to tell the stories that appear in these pages. I would also like to thank Ralph and Carolyn Curtis for generously opening their home and sharing their time and wisdom with me. If every person who worked in a prison were like them, prisons in this country would be a very different place. My father, who was a man of very few words, would say simply of Mr. and Mrs. Curtis, "good people," which would've been the highest praise.

The Government Department at Cornell, my professional home for the past twelve years, has been a wonderful place to explore what a forgiving society might look like. My colleagues in the department are enormously tolerant of the lawyer in their midst, and I would especially like to thank Jamila Michener and Mary Katzenstein, who patiently supported me as this book took shape. I also benefited from the research assistance of Kendra Candido, Sarah Rogers, and Dakota Stennett-Neris, former Cornell students who have since graduated and gone on to much better things but who taught me more than I taught them.

Val Bunce, Angela Douglas, Ann Gold, and David Levitsky read early drafts of various chapters and spared me from a number of embarrassing mistakes. Jim Goodman spent a great deal of time on the chapter about Richard Rivera, and his comments focused me when I needed it most. He made that chapter what it is. But when it comes to my writing, my greatest debt is to my good friend, Alex Kotlowitz. It was Alex who first suggested I write about forgiveness. He read every word of the manuscript, made scores of detailed suggestions that improved my work immeasurably, and repeatedly challenged me to think through the implications of my position. He does not agree with everything in this book, but more than anyone else, it bears his imprint.

I have long admired Beacon Press and am delighted to be one of their authors. The whole team at Beacon has been wonderful, but I was especially fortunate to work with Gayatri Patnaik, who pairs a great mind with a kind soul to produce an editor of rare skill. Bits and pieces of this book previously appeared in *Verdict*, where the publishers graciously provide me with the space to develop my ideas. Earlier versions of chapter 1 also appeared in *Boston Review* and *Inquest*. I am happy to recognize these three magazines and the talented trio of editors I have worked with for so many years: David Kemp at *Verdict*, Matt Lord at *Boston Review*, and Adam McGee at *Inquest*.

Finally, there is the debt for which language is pointless. I love the written word and write every day, but my pen fails me when I try to express what my wife, Sandra Babcock, means to me. She is everything and there is nothing else to write.

NOTES

INTRODUCTION

1. "CNN Gives Platform to Cartels," *The Ingraham Angle*, host Laura Ingraham, Fox News, May 5, 2025, www.foxnews.com.

CHAPTER 1: DISPATCH FROM A FORGIVING SOCIETY

1. Karen Crouse, "'I Let You Down': Klete Keller's Path from Olympics to Capitol Riot," *New York Times*, Jan. 19, 2021, https://www.nytimes.com/2021/01/18/sports/olympics/klete-keller-capitol-riot.html.

2. Tom Jackman, "Police Union Says 140 Officers Injured in Capitol Riot," *Washington Post*, Jan. 27, 2021, https://www.washingtonpost.com/local/public-safety/police-union-says-140-officers-injured-in-capitol-riot/2021/01/27/60743642-60e2-11eb-9430-e7c77b5b0297_story.html.

3. Alana Wise, "Capitol Police Officer Brian Sicknick Died of Natural Causes, Medical Examiner Rules," NPR, Apr. 19, 2021, https://www.npr.org/2021/04/19/988876722/capitol-police-officer-brian-sicknick-died-of-natural-causes-medical-examiner-ru; Peter Hermann, "D.C. Police Sent 850 Officers to the Capitol During Insurrection, Spent $8.8 Million During Week of Jan. 6," *Washington Post*, Jan. 26, 2021, https://www.washingtonpost.com/local/public-safety/contee-dcpolice-capitol-riot-/2021/01/26/8f386d12-6020-11eb-9061-07abcc1f9229_story.html; Evan Hill et al., "Video Shows How Rioter Was Trampled in Stampede at Capitol," *New York Times*, Jan. 15, 2021, https://www.nytimes.com/2021/01/16/us/politics/videos-show-how-a-rioter-was-trampled-in-the-stampede-at-the-capitol.html.

4. Michael McCullough, *Beyond Revenge: The Evolution of the Forgiveness Instinct* (Jossey-Bass, 2008), 162–75.

5. Michael McCullough et al., "Interpersonal Forgiving in Close Relationships," *Journal of Personality and Social Psychology* 73, no. 2 (1997): 321–36.

6. Jennifer L. Eberhardt et al., "Seeing Black: Race, Crime, and Visual Processing," *Journal of Personality & Social Psychology* 87 (2004): 876–93, https://psycnet.apa.org/record/2004-21339-010.

7. Tom Dreisbach and Meg Anderson, "Nearly 1 in 5 Defendants in Capitol Riot Cases Served in the Military," NPR, Jan. 21, 2021, https://www.npr.org/2021/01/21/958915267/nearly-one-in-five-defendants-in-capitol-riot-cases-served-in-the-military.

8. Tamar Walfisch et al., "Do You Really Expect Me to Apologize? The Impact of Status and Gender on the Effectiveness of an Apology in the Workplace," *Journal of Applied Social Psychology* 7, no. 43 (June 2013): 1446–58.

9. Carrie J. Petrucci, "Apology in the Criminal Justice Setting: Evidence for Including Apology as an Additional Component in the Legal System," *Behavioral Sciences & the Law* 20, no. 4 (July 2002): 337–62; Mark Tooley, "Elizabeth Bruenig on Forgiveness & Atonement," *Juicy Ecumenism*, July 13, 2020, https://juicyecumenism.com/2020/07/13/elizabeth-bruenig-interview/.

10. Michael Kunzelman, "Klete Keller, Olympic Gold Medalist Swimmer, Gets 6 Months in Home Detention for Jan. 6 Capitol Riot," AP News, updated Dec. 1, 2023, https://apnews.com/article/klete-keller-olympic-swimmer-capitol-riot-5d9767e13d2fb15c1d8ae2d04c99a12d.

CHAPTER 2: "THIS IS ERIC"

1. Joanne Ryan and Stephanie L. Perrault, "Angola: Plantation to Penitentiary," *Preserving Louisiana's Heritage*, no. 5, US Army Corps of Engineers (2007), https://www.crt.state.la.us/Assets/OCD/archaeology/discoverarchaeology/virtual-books/PDFs/Angola_Pop.pdf.

2. Martha Mahoney, "Law and Racial Geography: Public Housing and the Economy in New Orleans," *Stanford Law Review* 42, no. 5 (1990): 1251, 1271–72.

3. Mahoney, "Law and Racial Geography," 1280.

4. Stacy Seicshnaydre et al., *Rigging the Real Estate Market: Segregation, Inequality, and Disaster Risk*, Data Center, Apr. 2018, https://

s3.amazonaws.com/gnocdc/reports/TDC-prosperity-brief-stacy-seicshnaydre-et-al-FINAL.pdf; Mahoney, "Law and Racial Geography," 1257–60; see also Richard Rothstein, *The Color of Law: A Forgotten History of How Our Government Segregated America* (W. W. Norton, 2018).

5. Mahoney, "Law and Racial Geography," 1271, 1280; Shyam Gowtham, "How Longshoremen Built One of the Strongest Unions in America," *CrossDock Insights*, Oct. 10, 2024, https://crossdockinsights.com/p/who-are-the-longshoremen.

6. Natalia A. Kolesnikova and Yang Liu, "A Bleak 30 Years for Black Men: Economic Progress Was Slim in Urban America," Federal Reserve Bank of St. Louis, July 10, 2010, tables 1 and 3, https://www.stlouisfed.org/publications/regional-economist/july-2010/a-bleak-30-years-for-black-men-economic-progress-was-slim-in-urban-america.

7. Dan A. Black et al., "African-American Economic Progress in Urban Areas: A Tale of 14 American Cities," Federal Reserve Bank of St. Louis, June 2010, table 5, https://www.researchgate.net/publication/286461992_The_Economic_Progress_of_African_Americans_in_Urban_Areas_A_Tale_of_14_Cities.

8. Amund Rennesund Tallaksen, "Junkies and Jim Crow: Drugs, Race, and Incarceration in New Orleans, 1880–1980" (PhD diss., Carnegie Mellon University, 2015), 332.

9. Robert Habans et al., "The Origins and Persistence of Neighborhood Inequality," in *Placing Prosperity: Neighborhoods and Life Expectancy in the New Orleans Metro*, Data Center, Aug. 13, 2020, https://www.datacenterresearch.org/reports_analysis/placing-prosperity/; Wendall Rawls Jr., "Poverty Underlies New Orleans Veneer of Prosperity," *New York Times*, Sept. 8, 1980, https://www.nytimes.com/1980/09/08/archives/poverty-underlies-new-orleans-sheen-of-prosperity-well-keep-this.html.

10. Michael R. Geerken and Hennessey Hayes, *Crime in Greater New Orleans: Current Trends and Historical Patterns* (Sept. 1994): 7, https://www.ojp.gov/pdffiles1/Digitization/155214NCJRS.pdf.

11. "Tot's Murder Makes 7 in One Day for N.O.," *The Advocate* (Baton Rouge, LA), May 14, 1994, https://infoweb.newsbank.com/apps/news/document-view?p=AWNB&docref=news/0EB47790A1ECA0DF&f=basic.

12. Rawls, "Poverty Underlies New Orleans Veneer of Prosperity."

13. Tallaksen, "Junkies and Jim Crow," 332.

14. Demetrios Caraley, "Washington Abandons the Cities," *Political Science Quarterly* 107, no. 1 (Mar. 1992): 1–30.

15. Martha Burt, *Over the Edge: The Growth of Homelessness in the 1980s* (Russell Sage Foundation, 1992); Randy Shilts, *And the Band Played On: Politics, People, and the AIDS Epidemic* (St. Martin's Press, 1987); "DRUG ABUSE: The Crack Cocaine Epidemic: Health Consequences and Treatment," US General Accounting Office, Jan. 1991, https://www.gao.gov/assets/90/89031.pdf; Caraley, "Washington Abandons the Cities."

16. Mahoney, "Law and Racial Geography," 1280.

17. Tallaksen, "Junkies and Jim Crow," 201.

18. Habans et al., "The Origins and Persistence of Neighborhood Inequality."

19. Andrew Lang Golub and Bruce D. Johnson, "Crack's Decline: Some Surprises Across U.S. Cities," *Research in Brief*, National Institute of Justice, July 1997, https://www.ojp.gov/pdffiles/165707.pdf; Donovan X. Ramsey, *When Crack Was King: A People's History of a Misunderstood Era* (One World, 2023), 359.

20. Mary Foster, "Children Learn About Death Early in New Orleans' Projects," Associated Press, Oct. 27, 1992.

21. Jason DeParle, "Orphaned," *New York Times Magazine*, Aug. 27, 2006, https://www.nytimes.com/2006/08/27/magazine/27neworleans-1.html.

22. Foster, "Children Learn About Death Early in New Orleans' Projects."

23. Joy D. Osofsky, "The Impact of Violence on Children," *Future of Children* 9, no. 3 (Winter 1999): 36.

24. "Clinton Tells Story of Murdered Boy to Press Crime Bill's Passage," *Los Angeles Times*, July 17, 1994, https://www.latimes.com/archives/la-xpm-1994-07-17-mn-16816-story.html.

25. Bessel A. van der Kolk, *The Body Keeps the Score: Brain, Mind, and Body in the Healing of Trauma* (Penguin, 2014); Marilyn Metzler et al., "Adverse Childhood Experiences and Life Opportunities: Shifting the Narrative," *Children and Youth Services Review* 72 (Jan. 2017): 141–49, https://pmc.ncbi.nlm.nih.gov/articles/PMC10642285/.

26. Van der Kolk, *The Body Keeps the Score*; Metzler et al., "Adverse Childhood Experiences and Life Opportunities," 141–49.

27. Erin C. Dunn et al., "Is Developmental Timing of Trauma Exposure Associated with Depressive and Post-Traumatic Stress Disorder Symptoms in Adulthood?" *Journal of Psychiatric Research* 84 (Jan. 2017): 119–27, https://www.sciencedirect.com/science/article/abs/pii/S0022395616303430?via%3Dihub; Valerie J. Edwards et al., "Health Outcomes by Closeness of Sexual Abuse Perpetrator: A Test of Betrayal Trauma Theory," *Journal of Aggression, Maltreatment & Trauma* 21, no. 2 (Feb. 2012): 133–48, https://www.tandfonline.com/doi/full/10.1080/10926771.2012.648100?needAccess=true; Gayla Margolin, "Children's Exposure to Violence: Exploring Developmental Pathways to Diverse Outcomes," *Journal of Interpersonal Violence* 20, no. 1 (Feb. 2005): 72–81, https://www.researchgate.net/publication/8111276_Children's_Exposure_to_Violence.

28. Matthews v. Hooper, Application for Post-Conviction Relief, exbt. 2, Personal Statement of Eric Matthews.

29. Nadine Burke Harris, *The Deepest Well: Healing the Long-Term Effects of Childhood Adversity* (Houghton Mifflin Harcourt, 2018), 99, 108; Michael D. De Bellis and Abigail Zisk, "The Biological Effects of Childhood Trauma," *Child and Adolescent Psychiatric Clinics of North America* 23, no. 2 (Apr. 2014): 185–222, https://pmc.ncbi.nlm.nih.gov/articles/PMC3968319/; Osofsky, "The Impact of Violence on Children," 33; Bessel van der Kolk, "Posttraumatic Stress Disorder and the Nature of Trauma," *Posttraumatic Stress Disorder* 2, no. 1 (Apr. 2022): 7–22, https://pmc.ncbi.nlm.nih.gov/articles/PMC3181584/.

30. Vincent J. Felitti et al., "Relationship of Childhood Abuse and Household Dysfunction to Many of the Leading Causes of Death in Adults: The Adverse Childhood Experiences (ACE) Study," *Journal of Preventive Medicine* 14, no. 4 (May 1998): 245–58, https://www.ajpmonline.org/article/S0749-3797(98)00017-8/fulltext; Maxia Dong et al., "The Interrelatedness of Multiple Forms of Childhood Abuse, Neglect, and Household Dysfunction," *Child Abuse & Neglect* 28, no. 7 (July 2004): 771–84, https://www.researchgate.net/publication/8449077_The_interrelatedness_of_multiple_forms_of_childhood_abuse_neglect_and_household_dysfunction.

31. *Matthews v. Hooper*, Application for Post-Conviction Relief.

32. *Matthews v. Hooper*, Application for Post-Conviction Relief.

33. *Matthews v. Hooper*, Application for Post-Conviction Relief.

34. "The Prison Seminary Model," Prison Seminaries Foundation, n.d., https://www.prisonseminaries.org/the-prison-seminary-model.

35. The Sentencing Project, *People Serving Life Exceeds Entire Prison Population of 1970*, Feb. 20, 2020, https://www.sentencingproject.org/reports/people-serving-life-exceeds-entire-prison-population-of-1970/; Ashley Nellis and Celeste Barry, *A Matter of Life: The Scope and Impact of Life and Long Term Imprisonment in the United States*, The Sentencing Project, Jan. 8, 2025, https://www.sentencingproject.org/reports/a-matter-of-life-the-scope-and-impact-of-life-and-long-term-imprisonment-in-the-united-states/.

36. Nellis and Barry, *A Matter of Life*.

37. Lydia Pelot-Hobbs, "The Contested Terrain of the Louisiana Carceral State: Dialectics of Southern Penal Expansion, 1971–2016" (PhD diss., City University of New York, 2019), 93.

38. Pelot-Hobbs, "The Contested Terrain of the Louisiana Carceral State," 94.

CHAPTER 3: "WHAT THE FUCK IS WRONG WITH THIS KID?"

1. Jennifer Gonnerman, "The Supermax Solution," *Village Voice*, May 18, 1999, https://www.villagevoice.com/the-supermax-solution/.

2. Katja Lane, ed., *Deceived, Damned and Defiant: The Revolutionary Writings of David Lane* (14 Word Press), 5–6.

3. Ron McVan, *Creed of Iron: Wotansvolk Wisdom* (14 Word Press), 44.

4. Ben Klassen, *The White Man's Bible* (Creativity Book Publishers, 1981), 413.

5. See, e.g., Alexander Meleagrou-Hitchens et al., "Rise of the Reactionaries: Comparing the Ideologies of Salafi-Jihadism and White Supremacist Extremism," George Washington University Program on Extremism, Dec. 2021, https://extremism.gwu.edu/sites/g/files/zaxdzs5746/files/Rise%20of%20the%20Reactionaries.pdf.

6. Debbie M. Price, "In Upstate New York, Leather's Long Shadow," *Undark*, Feb. 22, 2017, https://undark.org/2017/02/22/leathers-long-shadow-gloversville-new-york/.

7. C. S. Lewis, *The Problem of Pain* (Adage Books, 2021), 136.

8. You can watch the scene on YouTube, https://www.youtube.com/watch?v=SIYkhb2NjfE.

9. See, e.g., Anti-Defamation League, "White Supremacists Embrace 'Race War,'" Jan. 8, 2020, https://www.adl.org/resources/blog/white-supremacists-embrace-race-war.

10. See Tom Robbins, "Attica's Ghosts," The Marshall Project, Feb. 28, 2015, https://www.themarshallproject.org/2015/02/28/attica-s-ghosts; John J. Lennon, "Spying on Attica," The Marshall Project, Apr. 9, 2018, https://www.themarshallproject.org/2018/04/09/spying-on-attica.

11. Joseph Maher, "Cook, Whaley Sentenced for Murder—Judge Says Both Men 'Lucked Out' Because of Age," *Schenectady Gazette*, Feb. 23, 1999, https://infoweb.newsbank.com/apps/news/document-view?p=AWNB&docref=news/1110FF68EAA918D3&f=basic.

CHAPTER 4: "THE DISQUIETING COMPLEXITY OF OURSELVES"

1. I was one of Lisa's lawyers in her last appeals, but was not among the lawyers who met her. Except where otherwise noted, the facts presented in this chapter are drawn from the reports of Dr. Katherine Porterfield, a psychologist with an expertise in survivors of child sexual abuse, and Jan Vogelsang, a clinical social worker, both of whom spent hours interviewing Lisa and her neighbors, friends, and family. Their reports were prepared before I became involved in the case.

2. *United States v. Lisa Montgomery*, trial transcript (TT), vol. 8, 1730.

3. Physicians for Human Rights, "Module 6: Psychological Evidence of Torture and Ill-Treatment," Tools & Resources, accessed March 2, 2026.

4. Clare MacMartin and A. Daniel Yarmey, "Rhetoric and the Recovered Memory Debate," *Canadian Psychology* 40, no. 4 (November 1999): 343–58.

5. Rebecca Bailey et al., "Appeasement: Replacing Stockholm Syndrome as a Definition of a Survival Strategy," *European Journal of Psychotraumatology* 14, no. 1 (Jan. 2023): 216, https://pubmed.ncbi.nlm.nih.gov/37052112/; Chris Cantor and John Price, "Traumatic Entrapment, Appeasement and Complex Post-Traumatic Stress Disorder: Evolutionary Perspectives of Hostage Reactions, Domestic Abuse and the Stockholm Syndrome," *Australian & New Zealand Journal of Psychiatry* 41, no. 5 (May 2007): 377–84.

6. E.g., TT, vol. 6, 1520.

7. *United States v. Lisa Montgomery*, Federal Evidentiary Hearing (FH), vol. 9, 2351.

8. FH, vol. 6, 1516.

9. TT, vol. 8, 1825–26; TT, vol. 5, 1091; TT, vol. 8, 1843; TT, vol. 8, 1858–59; TT, vol. 8, 1868–70.

10. E.g., TT, vol. 8, 1738, 1742.

11. TT, 3189, 3155, 3165, 3184.

12. James Baldwin, *Everybody's Protest Novel: Essays* (1955; repr. Beacon Press, 2024), 5.

13. Baldwin, *Everybody's Protest Novel*, 6.

CHAPTER 5: "WHAT IF IT'S JUST HUMAN BEINGS?"

1. Alexandre Marchant, "The French Connection: Between Myth and Reality," *Vingtième Siècle. Revue d'histoire* 115 (2012–2013): 89–102, https://shs.cairn.info/journal-vingtieme-siecle-revue-d-histoire-2012-3-page-89?lang=en.

2. Leslie Soble et al., *Eating Behind Bars: Ending the Hidden Punishment of Food in Prison*, Impact Justice, 2020, https://impactjustice.org/wp-content/uploads/IJ-Eating-Behind-Bars.pdf.

3. Soble et al., *Eating Behind Bars*; Correctional Association of New York, *Food Access and Quality in New York Prisons*, 2021, https://static1.squarespace.com/static/62f1552c1dd65741c53bbcf8/t/6318edc3b84b176199698e7e/1678304102660/2021_FoodAccessandQuality.pdf.

4. Wendy Sawyer, "How Much Do Incarcerated People Earn in Each State?" *Prison Policy Initiative* (blog), Apr. 10, 2017, https://www.prisonpolicy.org/blog/2017/04/10/wages/; ACLU, *Captive Labor: Exploitation of Incarcerated Workers*, with Global Human Rights Clinic, University of Chicago Law School, June 15, 2022, https://assets.aclu.org/live/uploads/publications/2022-06-15-captivelaborresearchreport.pdf; Freddy Medina, "Inflation Is Putting Food Out of Reach in NY Prisons," *NY Focus*, Apr. 11, 2023, https://nysfocus.com/2023/04/11/prison-package-ban-inflation-hunger.

5. Elizabeth Weill-Greenberg and Ethan Corey, "Locked In, Priced Out: How Prison Commissary Price-Gouging Preys on the Incarcerated," *The Appeal*, Apr. 17, 2024, https://theappeal.org/locked-in-priced-out-how-much-prison-commissary-prices/.

6. Tiana Herring, "COVID Looks Like It May Stay. That Means Prison Medical Copays Must Go," *Prison Policy Initiative* (blog), Feb. 1, 2022, https://www.prisonpolicy.org/blog/2022/02/01/pandemic_copays/#appendices.

7. Prison Policy Initiative, *State of Phone Justice, 2022*, "Appendix Table 1: Phone Rates for 15-Minute Increments in State Prisons, 2008–2021," 2022, https://www.prisonpolicy.org/phones/appendices2022_1.html; Tommaso Bardelli et al., "Surviving Austerity:

Commissary Stores, Inequality and Punishment in the Contemporary American Prison," *Punishment and Society* 25, no. 4 (Aug. 2022): 1–22, https://www.researchgate.net/publication/362557387_Surviving_austerity_Commissary_stores_inequality_and_punishment_in_the_contemporary_American_prison.

8. Richard Rivera, "I Survived Prison During the AIDS Epidemic. Here's What It Taught Me About Coronavirus," The Marshall Project, May 14, 2020, https://www.themarshallproject.org/2020/05/14/i-survived-prison-during-the-aids-epidemic-here-s-what-it-taught-me-about-coronavirus.

9. Adam Gopnik, "Learning from the Slaughter in Attica," *New Yorker*, Aug. 22, 2016, https://www.newyorker.com/magazine/2016/08/29/learning-from-the-slaughter-in-attica; see also Asha Bandele, "After the Attica Uprising," *The Nation*, Sept. 9, 2011, https://www.thenation.com/article/archive/after-attica-uprising/.

10. Quoted in Mariame Kaba, *Attica Prison Uprising 101: A Short Primer*, Project NIA, Sept. 2011, https://project-nia.org/uploads/documents/Educational-Curricula/Attica%20Prison%20Uprising%20101.pdf.

11. Monica Moorehead, "L. D. Barkley—A Leader in the Attica Uprising," *Workers World* (blog), Feb. 17, 2021, https://www.workers.org/2021/02/54535/; Attica Prison Liberation Faction, Manifesto of Demands, Sept. 9, 1971, https://libcom.org/article/attica-prison-liberation-faction-manifesto-demands-1971.

12. Pam Widener, "Eddie Ellis at Large," *Prison Life*, Oct. 1996, https://www.prisonlegalnews.org/media/publications/Prison_Life_October_1996.pdf#page=49; Orisanmi Burton, "Eddie Ellis and the Struggle for Black Freedom," *Counterpunch*, Aug. 8, 2014, quoting Ellis in unpublished conversation with Dr. Muhammad Ahmad, https://www.counterpunch.org/2014/08/08/eddie-ellis-and-the-struggle-for-black-freedom/; Nathaniel Sheppard, "Green Haven Reports Increase in Prisoner Clashes," *New York Times*, Nov. 2, 1976, https://www.nytimes.com/1976/11/02/archives/green-haven-reports-increase-in-prisoner-clashes.html.

13. National Research Council (US) Panel on Monitoring the Social Impact of the AIDS Epidemic, "Correctional Systems," in *The Social Impact of AIDS in the United States*, ed. A. R. Jonsen and J. Stryker (National Academies Press, 1993), 7: Correctional Systems, https://www.ncbi.nlm.nih.gov/books/NBK234573/.

14. Jessica Lee, "Is Man Who Killed Cop in '81 Helping NY Officials Reform Policing?" Snopes, Apr. 1, 2021, https://www.snopes.com/fact-check/cop-killer-police-reform/.

CHAPTER 6: "HE'S NOT READY"

1. Ken Raymond, "Oklahoma City Faces Growing Gang Problem," *The Oklahoman*, July 6, 2003, https://www.oklahoman.com/story/news/2003/07/06/oklahoma-city-faces-growing-gang-problem/62036271007/.

2. Raymond, "Oklahoma City Faces Growing Gang Problem"; National Drug Intelligence Center, *North Texas: High Intensity Drug Trafficking Area: Drug Market Analysis*, US Department of Justice, 2008, p. 15, https://www.justice.gov/archive/ndic/pubs27/27503/27503p.pdf.

3. Ken Raymond, "After Last Summer's Gang Violence, Police and Everyday Citizens Worked Together to Make the Streets Safer," *The Oklahoman*, Aug. 15, 2004, https://www.oklahoman.com/story/news/2004/08/15/summers-violence-everyday-citizens-worked-together-streets-activity-oklahoma-readybrsomething-happen/61978451007/; Raymond, "Oklahoma City Faces Growing Gang Problem"; Associated Press, "Drive-by Shooting Leaves 9-Year-Old Dead in Oklahoma City," News On 6, Aug. 11, 2004, https://www.newson6.com/story/5e367d932f69d76f62090ca8/driveby-shooting-leaves-9yearold-dead-in-oklahoma-city; "Getting a Grip: Many Hands Needed to Help Curb Gang Activity," editorial, *The Oklahoman*, Sept. 6, 2007, https://www.oklahoman.com/story/news/2007/09/06/getting-a-grip-many-hands-needed-to-curb-gang-activity/61721971007/.

4. Ty McMahan, "Jury Acquits Men in Drive-by Shooting," *The Oklahoman*, Dec. 9, 2005, https://www.oklahoman.com/story/news/2005/12/09/jury-acquits-men-in-drive-by-killing/61911542007/.

5. Ken Raymond, "65 Arrested on Warrants. Agencies Work Together to Nab Gang Members," *The Oklahoman*, Oct. 16, 2004, https://www.oklahoman.com/story/news/2004/10/16/65-arrested-on-warrantsbragencies-work-together-to-nab-gang-members/61970203007/.

6. Joe Wertz, "City Sees Rise in Drive-by Shootings: Warring Gangs' Deadly Gunfights over Turf Often Blamed, Police Say," *The Oklahoman*, Sept. 20, 2006, https://www.oklahoman.com/story/news/crime/2006/09/20/city-sees-rise-in-drive-by-shootings/61857954007/.

7. Quoted in Christopher M. Hill et al., *Evaluation of the Oklahoma City Gang and Violent Crime Program*, Oklahoma State Bureau

of Investigation and Oklahoma City Police Department, June 9–10, 2010, https://oklahoma.gov/content/dam/ok/en/osbi/documents/sac-documents/evaluations/Evaluation_of_the_Oklahoma_City_Gang_and_Violent_Crime_Program_June_2010.pdf.

8. Justice.gov, "Prepared Remarks of Attorney General Alberto R. Gonzales on Efforts to Combat Gang Violence in Oklahoma City," May 1, 2007, https://www.justice.gov/archive/ag/speeches/2007/ag_speech_0705015.html; Centers for Disease Control and Prevention, "Gang Homicides—Five U.S. Cities: 2003–2008," *Morbidity and Mortality Weekly Report* 61, no. 3 (Jan. 27, 2012): 46–51, https://www.cdc.gov/mmwr/preview/mmwrhtml/mm6103a2.htm.

9. First quote: Trial transcript, State of Texas v. Ted Calvin Cole, no. CR88-0043-A (Tx. Ct. Crim. App Jan. 11, 1989), vol. 17, p. 767, Testimony of Dr. Richard Coons. Second quote: Trial transcript, United States v. Bruce Corneil Webster, 4: 94-CR-121-4 (N. D. Tx Jun. 18, 1996), vol. 26, pp. 154–55, Testimony of Dr. Richard Coons.

CHAPTER 7: "HE IS NOT THAT PERSON TODAY"

1. S. P. Davis, "Survey: Some States Save Millions Using Inmate Labor to Build Prisons," *Corrections Compendium* 15, no. 7 (Sept. 1990): 8–17, 19, https://www.ojp.gov/ncjrs/virtual-library/abstracts/survey-some-states-save-millions-using-inmate-labor-build-prisons.

2. Celina Aldape et al., *Rethinking Death Row: Variations in the Housing of Individuals Sentenced to Death*, Arthur Liman Public Interest Program, Yale Law School, July 2016, https://law.yale.edu/sites/default/files/documents/pdf/Liman/deathrow_reportfinal.pdf.

3. Monica Obradovic, "Brian Dorsey Killed 2 People. Now He's Fighting to Avoid Execution," *River Front Times*, Jan. 18, 2024.

4. Tiah Shepherd, "Missouri Gov. Rejects Prison Guards' Calls to Stop Execution of Brian Dorsey," *The Hill*, Apr. 8, 2024, https://thehill.com/homenews/4581966-missouri-gov-rejects-prison-guards-calls-to-stop-execution-of-brian-dorsey/.

CHAPTER 8: THE WHATABOUTS

1. Tovia Smith, "Conspiracy Theorist Alex Jones Accused of Hiding Money from Sandy Hook Families," NPR, June 18, 2025, https://www.wuft.org/2025-06-18/conspiracy-theorist-alex-jones-accused-of-hiding-money-from-sandy-hook-families.

2. American Psychological Association, "Why Some People Are Willing to Believe Conspiracy Theories," news release, June 26, 2023, https://www.apa.org/news/press/releases/2023/06/why-people-believe-conspiracy-theories; Shauna M. Bowes et al., "The Conspiratorial Mind: A Meta-Analytic Review of Motivational and Personological Correlates," *Psychological Bulletin* 149, no. 5–6 (May–June 2023): 259–93, https://psycnet.apa.org/record/2023-79252-001.

3. Bowes et al., "The Conspiratorial Mind."

4. CBS News, "Sandy Hook Conspiracy Theorist Sentenced for Threat," June 8, 2017, https://www.cbsnews.com/news/sandy-hook-shooting-conspiracy-theorist-sentenced-threat/.

THE WAY FORWARD

1. Rick Maese, "Olympian Klete Keller, Pardoned by Trump, Expresses 'Regret' for Jan. 6," *Washington Post*, Jan. 21, 2025, https://www.washingtonpost.com/sports/olympics/2025/01/21/klete-keller-jan-6-olympic-swimmer-trump/.

ABOUT THE AUTHOR

Joseph Margulies long ago distilled his personal philosophy to eight words: "There is no them; there is only us." A writer and litigator, as well as a Professor of the Practice of Government at Cornell University, he is opposed to demonization in all its forms and does not believe in the "other." All of his work—as a lawyer, writer, and teacher—takes aim at the real and imagined walls we build to separate "us" from "them."

As a civil rights lawyer, he was counsel in *Rasul v. Bush* in 2004, which gave Guantánamo detainees the right to challenge their detention in federal court; in *Munaf v. Geren* in 2008, which gave American citizens the right to challenge their detention by the US government, even if they are imprisoned in foreign war zones; and in *United States v. Abu Zubaydah* in 2022, where the Supreme Court recognized that the so-called enhanced interrogations used by the CIA after September 11, 2001, were torture. He is also the director of the Compassionate Release Project, which represents people held in federal prisons in motions to reduce their sentence.

Margulies is the author of numerous articles and three other books: *Thanks for Everything, Now Get Out: Can We Restore Neighborhoods Without Destroying Them?* (Yale, 2021); *What Changed When Everything Changed: 9/11 and the Making of National Identity* (Yale, 2013); and *Guantánamo and the Abuse of Presidential Power* (Simon & Schuster, 2006), which won several awards. He lives in Upstate New York.